THE BIKER'S GUIDE TO TEXAS

To my three wonderful daughters
Melissa
Madeline
Melanie
Enjoy the ride!

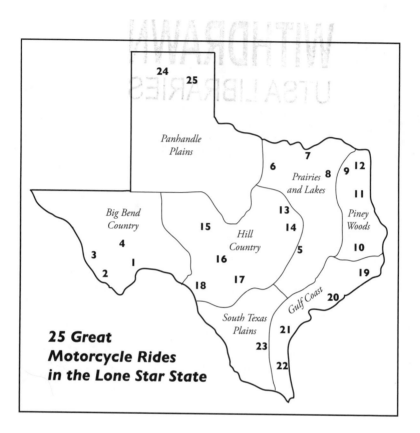

Panhandle
Plains

24
25

7

6

Prairies
and Lakes

8 9 12

11

Big Bend
Country

15

13

14

Piney
Woods

4

3

1

16

Hill
Country

5

10

2

18

17

19

Gulf Coast

20

South Texas
Plains

21

**25 Great
Motorcycle Rides
in the Lone Star State**

23

22

The Biker's Guide to Texas

25 Great Motorcycle Rides in the Lone Star State

Dorothy Waldman

MAVERICK PUBLISHING COMPANY

Maverick Publishing Company
P. O. Box 6355, San Antonio, Texas 78209

Library of Congress Cataloging-in-Publication Data

Waldman, Dorothy.
    The biker's guide to Texas : 25 great motorcycle rides in the Lone Star State /
Dorothy Waldman.
        p. cm.
Includes index.
    ISBN 1-893271-36-6 (alk. paper)
    1. Motorcycle touring–Texas–Guidebooks. 2. Texas–Guidebooks. I. Title.
    GV1059.522.T4W35 2005
    917.6404'64–dc22

                                                              2005015294

5 4 3 2 1

Map routes by Judi Burton Design.
Cover photo by Craig Weisiger. Unattributed photos by the author.

Contents

How to Have Fun Riding

"How do you know where to ride?" I asked the friend who first intro-duced me to motorcycles.

"You talk to people and experiment a lot," he responded. "And then you ride a lot of roads that aren't great and get lost."

Frankly, that did not sound like a lot of fun to me. As much as I loved riding, I did not like the idea of wasting the few precious hours I had each week for pleasure riding getting lost on not-great roads when another, fantastic route was nearby. As a new rider, I still needed to concentrate on my riding and road conditions rather than worrying about getting back before search parties came after me. My crazy schedule as a writer and speaker rarely matched up with organized rides, so I was left to my own limited sense of geography to figure out where to ride.

There was only one thing to do: write the guidebook I wanted to use. But as a new rider, I needed a lot of help.

Obviously, the best roads are in less-densely populated areas. But these are also the places where there are the fewest roads and the least accurate mapping and signs. You might go miles to figure out that, after a wrong turn, you're not headed in the direction you want to go.

As I talked to bikers, even to very experienced riders, I realized that others had the same concerns. No one ever complained about having too much time to ride. Everyone was as crunched for time as I was, yet all wanted to have as much fun as possible every precious minute on that bike. For many, that meant traveling on the same roads to eliminate the stress of getting lost and wandering around unknown territory.

Some people love the thrill of endless, blind wandering. It does take you to new places, and you never know when you will accidentally come across the road of a lifetime that no one else has ever explored. But for me, that scenario spells stress. I agree that a lot of the fun is just being on the bike and riding and that the destination is not always the goal; it's the getting there. However, I want to return safely to familiar terri-tory with a minimal amount of trauma.

Other people I talked to tended to ride mainly on the major roads. One advantage is the consistency. An Interstate or a US highway is always going to be among the best maintained. Hills and curves will always be gentle, and there will always be a wide shoulder. The downside to an Interstate or a US highway is that there will be traffic, there will always be construction or repairs being made somewhere, and you will miss one of the best parts of biking—being free and alone on a great road.

Taking organized rides headed by an experienced leader who knows the great roads is one way a lot of riders learn where to go. Group rides are fine as long as your schedule can accommodate the set times of the rides and as long as they go where you want to when you want to. And although traveling with a large pack of bikers is a lot of fun and there is safety in numbers, it is still a large-group activity.

But at some point, every biker wants to hit the road alone or with just a few choice friends. *The Biker's Guide to Texas* has twenty-five fantastic rides in all areas of the state, so you can go where you want to when you want to.

My first goal is to give good directions, so that even someone who is "geographically challenged" can follow them and not get lost in the process. As simple as that may sound, considering the craziness of some Texas roads and the lack of signs in many areas, it is a real challenge.

Also, bikers need to find their way back home at the end of a ride. That is why many of these rides are circular, starting and stopping at the same place—but with little or no backtracking. On some trips, like the Lindbergh Legacy from New York to Paris, the ride follows scenic farm-to-market roads. Directions are given to US 75, the closest major highway. Then you can travel back to wherever you want to go, since I'm almost positive no one doing this ride is based out of New York, Texas.

Most rides, such as those in West Texas, can be done individually or strung together to make a long, multi-day, or killer-day ride. For the circle rides, especially, it does not matter where you begin or end the trip. Just follow the directions.

My next goal is to communicate what a rider can expect along the way, by way of road conditions such as number of lanes, sharpness of curves, steepness of grade, and anything else that could affect the thrill of the ride and the necessary level of expertise. Many routes rely on farm-to-market (FM) roads, ranch roads (RR) and even some county roads (CR). Travel these roads at your own risk.

This book also includes notes on what the countryside looks like and on special or unique places to eat, sleep, or sightsee. Larger towns and cities tend to have a full repertoire of familiar goods and services, including plenty of facilities for eating, sleeping, and fueling. Included here are those that are more interesting than the typical franchise establishment. Of course, if you see a parking lot filled with bikes, it's probably a safe bet that it is a good place to stop.

All this information is to help you have fun. If you know where you're going, how to get there and back again, what to see, and where to stop along the way, the trip will be fun.

The most important part of riding fun is riding safely. If a ride is more than you or your companion can handle, save it for when you're up to it. Use your best judgment as to what you are capable of and how much you want to do in any given day.

Although I'm not your mother, wife, or guardian angel, I feel strongly about the need to follow basic safety precautions. That includes following all speed limits and laws and practicing safe-riding techniques. You are responsible for your own safety. The one precaution I feel most strongly about is wearing a helmet. I know a number of people who are still riding today because a helmet saved their lives. That includes the friend who introduced me to this sport.

If you do go off somewhere by yourself, be sure to let someone know your planned route and when you expect to return, just in case you don't. It's also a good idea to carry a cell phone with you, along with some drinks, food, and rain gear. You never know when the famous Texas weather will make a sudden change. And, like when you operate any machinery, use discretion when consuming alcohol or taking any sort of medicines or drugs. This book is no substitute for common sense.

As good friend and motorcycle enthusiast Jerry Sun says, "It is better at times to ride with caution and be thought unskilled than to ride with speed and remove all doubt."

So why are you sitting here reading a book?

Let's RIDE!

Getting Started

Motorcycles are the stuff fantasies are made of. After dreaming of taking off for the wild blue yonder, now is your chance to transform your fantasy into a reality.

First, get the feel of where you want to go. Some rides may be close to home; you might want to try something nearby first. Of course, the familiar is never as exotic as new territory. If you want to branch off to new routes and roads, the rides in this book can act as your personal guide to the great unknown.

Many rides have suggestions for variations and detours, so you can customize your ride to suit your interests and the amount of time you have to live out your fantasy. Many stops are listed, and more can be found on the official site of Texas tourism, www.TravelTex.com. If something strikes your fancy, make that your destination, and enjoy. In most cases there will be something of interest often enough to make even mandatory pit stops and butt breaks fun.

One thing all bikers have in common is that they like to ride. Sometimes you like to have a definitive destination, if for no other reason than to know when to turn around to go back. The truth is that if sightseeing were the main purpose, there would be no reason to ride. As motorcycle riders know, the main destination is the bike itself and the open road. That is the emphasis of this book.

There are plenty of books that tell you where to stop; this book tells you where to ride.

All of the mileage listed is a close approximation to reality. Yours may vary a little. Road conditions are those at the time I took the route. A massive meteor shower or ignored wear and tear can create potholes and other hazards over night. Lights, signs and other marks of civilization, including road and commercial construction, come and go, especially near cities and resort areas. If Mega Merger, Inc. decides to build its Universal Outlet and Headquarters on former ranchland just outside of Lajitas, the area won't match my descriptions.

A word about state parks. Many rides in this book come in close proximity to one of the many Texas state parks because those are located in places where something special makes the land worth preserving in its natural state. Even if you elect not to take the detour into a specific park, by being nearby you'll still get some idea of what made the land worth preserving.

However, if you do decide to tour the park, you'll be rewarded. Each park is unique in its own way and offers its own special programs. If you find you're drawn to rides that go by parks and are tempted to turn in, consider getting a Texas State Parks Pass, which gives you unlimited visits to all 120 state parks and historic sites in Texas as well as other benefits at a very reasonable cost. Information on the parks and the pass is available at www.tpwd.state.tx.us.

When you're in a state park, be sure to follow the rules: speed limits, riding only on designated roadways, and all the others. Always respect others in the parks; the parks belong to everyone. Bikers are no longer considered the hellions they once were; don't spoil your good name.

Big Bend Country

For most Texans, trekking to West Texas to ride is a major ordeal. But once you actually start riding, you will realize it is worth all the trouble and hassles of getting here. Nowhere else in the state can you ride so high and so close to the sky that you can almost reach out and touch heaven. Nowhere else can you go for as long and have as much riding pleasure as you can in West Texas. Nowhere else does the blue sky totally surround and envelop you in a cocoon of excitement and pure riding ecstasy.

West Texas still has the look and feel of the Wild West of the old Roy Rogers or John Wayne movies. As your eyes scan the distant horizon and the flat purple tops of towering mesas, you can almost see the lone Indian scout on horseback searching out interlopers galloping through the uninhabited territory. The rocky hills and scrub-brush covered pastures all look vaguely familiar because of the television westerns you have seen.

Here are three mountain rides through West Texas. They can be ridden individually or linked together to form one long, adventurous trip. However, trying to do all three in one day is a feat that only experts and iron butts should attempt. Instead, take a couple of days, stop often, and enjoy the sights. Or come back later on another trip to finish up the entire series. Because not everyone can spend a week riding all the wonderful West Texas roads, even if that is the dream, a shorter ride that includes some of the best roads is also included.

Since this area is part of the Texas Mountain Trail, keep in mind that the winters can be cold, at least for those Texans used to warmer climes. The summers are merely cool, especially at higher elevations. On the descent from the mountaintops, temperatures change considerably. Remember the old joke about Texas weather: "If you don't like it, wait a minute." The temps fluctuate according to the altitude. So be prepared with layers of clothing you can either add or take off.

Also be sure you begin each ride with a full tank of fuel, plenty of water, some snacks, and a cell phone. These rides feature a lot of wide-open spaces between bikes, provisions, fuel, and other signs of civilization. Your cell phone may not work in places. There is generally not much traffic, so you cannot count on immediately being able to flag down a passing vehicle if you need help, although someone will almost always pass by within a few hours.

Ride 1: Touching Heaven
The Mountainous Route between Kent and Study Butte

This ride follows a stretch of the Texas Mountain Trail that takes you on some of the best mountain roads you can imagine. Not only will you go over hills and around corkscrew curves but you will also see some of the most beautiful landscapes in Texas. Everything in this part of the state is bigger, farther, and longer than anywhere else. The sky and ranches are bigger, going on for miles further than you thought possible. The distances are further, so be sure to top off your tank whenever you get the chance.

Kent, Texas, is the perfect starting point for a grand ride that will take you through some of the most majestic scenery anywhere. Your biggest complaint may be that you can't enjoy it as much as you would like because you have to pay attention to the even better riding. Take the road easy so you can do both, enjoy the ride and enjoy the countryside.

Since there is so much territory to cover, start early in the morning before the temperatures get too high. It might also take you a while to get to Kent, the starting point for this ride. Kent is at the intersection of I-10W and TX 118, a little more than eighty miles of flat straight riding due west from Fort Stockton. However you get to Kent, turn south and begin the ride of a lifetime.

This ride stops at the McDonald Observatory, where your eyes can literally reach out to the celestial limits of the universe. The route then brings you back to earth at the frontier town that sprang up around Fort Davis and still cherishes its Wild West roots. Between the sparse towns there is a lot of exhilarating riding and great panoramas. For some reason, the sky seems bluer and bigger here than anywhere else in the state.

The Touching Heaven Ride ends in Study Butte, just a hop, skip, and a jump from Big Bend National Park. The roads in Big Bend are well marked and are also thrilling to ride with beautiful scenery. Some bikers live for their excursions into the park. Others avoid them because they consider the speed limits, which are strictly enforced, too low for full riding enjoyment of the territory. Do what suits you best. No matter what you decide, it's hard not to have a good ride around here.

Getting Started: Kent to McDonald Observatory

Kent was founded as a water stop for the Texas and Pacific Railroad in the 1880s. The town is still remote, even though I-10, a major east-west thoroughfare across the state, runs through it. TX 118, heading south from Kent, is a two-lane state highway through the Davis Mountains, with lots of deep curves going around, up, and down one mountain. After a brief straightaway, the curves and hills begin again up the next incline. The road goes up and around the mountains, not through, then in and out of valleys.

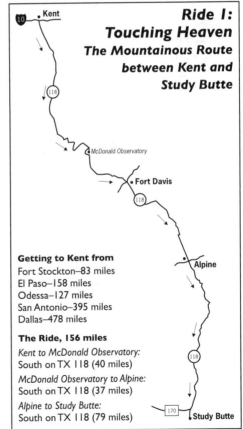

Fortunately, there are places to pull over to the side so you can safely enjoy the vastness of the beautiful vistas. Sometimes it's hard to appreciate fully the surrounding scenery when you have to concentrate on riding the road.

The posted speed limit in this area is 75 mph, realistic for the normal driving conditions on the long flat stretches. So when a sign warns of a series of corkscrew curves ahead with a lower speed limit, believe it. In fact, at times the speed limits seem to be geared toward the na-

Ride 1:
Touching Heaven
The Mountainous Route between Kent and Study Butte

Getting to Kent from
Fort Stockton–83 miles
El Paso–158 miles
Odessa–127 miles
San Antonio–395 miles
Dallas–478 miles

The Ride, 156 miles
Kent to McDonald Observatory:
South on TX 118 (40 miles)
McDonald Observatory to Alpine:
South on TX 118 (37 miles)
Alpine to Study Butte:
South on TX 118 (79 miles)

tives who have "local knowledge" and are familiar with the twists and turns of the pavement, not toward tourist bikers who are riding the roads for the first time. If you are not an expert in this type of riding and are unfamiliar with the area, take the curves with caution, or, better yet, ride at a moderate speed so you can safely enjoy the glorious scenery.

On a clear day—and most days are clear—you can see Van Horn Mountain sixty miles away. Watch for the sign pointing it out when you are approximately twenty-three miles south of Kent.

Miles of fences line both sides of the road. Vast ranches dominate the area. With the normal arid conditions, a lot of acreage is needed to support a herd of cattle. However, you might go miles without seeing a single cow. Or you might see large herds clustered together by the side of a fence chowing down on the vegetation.

After TX 166 branches off from TX 118, the road becomes a bit narrower, with no shoulders and even more sharp curves. A double yellow line down the middle of the road is there for a reason: you won't be going 75 mph around these curves, and you won't be passing. This ride is not suited for weak stomachs or faint hearts. When the posted speed limit is 35 mph going around a series of sharp corkscrew curves, believe that is reasonable. If you're a good rider and exercise sensible caution, you will do fine and have a great, safe time.

This is also a road not to take in the rain. "Watch for Water on Road" signs appear at dips and low places. Fortunately for bikers, though not necessarily for the locals, rain does not fall much here. The plethora of cactus in the fields attests to that.

At Spur 8, turn east to go to the McDonald Observatory, which is run by a consortium of five universities from around the world. The altitude at the observatory is close to 7,000 feet, so the grade up to the huge domes that house the vast telescopes is quite steep. You will ride the steepest roads in Texas right here. Coming out of the observatory be prepared to use your gears, and maybe even your brakes. One steep, sharp, slow corkscrew follows another, all the way down. The speed limit to the area with two telescopes on the self-guided tour is 30 mph. The speed limit to the mountaintop with the third scope is 15 mph. These limits may actually be a bit generous for bikers.

Mount Locke was chosen as the site for the observatory because of the clear air, high ratio of cloudless nights, distance from concentrations

Moonrise over the McDonald Observatory on Mount Locke.

of artificial ground lights, and dust-and radiation-filtering growths of shrubs and timber. The third-largest telescope in the world is located here. There are day solar-viewing programs in the summer as well as guided and self-guided tours. In addition there are night programs if you want to return in the evening

All along this ride you might pass or meet bicyclists struggling to conquer the challenging terrain. Be kind to them as you fly by, leaving them in the wake of your exhaust.

McDonald Observatory to Alpine

By this time, you have had enough practice to become skilled at taking the sharp turns and curves. You have learned that if the recommended speed limit is 50 mph, you are probably facing a relatively easy curve compared to other curves with lower limits. Even so, don't get too cocky and sure of yourself and do anything foolish. Enjoy the pleasure of the ride.

The next fifteen miles to Fort Davis are pure riding ecstasy. Looking toward the mountains, you can see the road zigzagging ahead. The best part is you know that this is a preview of where you will be soon. The tops of the mountains are lined with rock formations that look like petrified centurions standing guard. The landscape gets rockier and more rugged the farther south you go. All along this part of the ride the views are huge and magnificent. Fortunately, there are roadside rest areas where you can stop to enjoy the great vastness of the vistas as well as prepare yourself for the next stretch of challenging riding.

Fort Davis is an excellent place to stop and spend a little time because there is so much to do and see here. Looking like an updated version of the Old West, Fort Davis has a number of places to sleep and eat. Bikers are a frequent and welcomed sight here, sort of the modern version of the free spirits who passed through in the past.

Pioneers and gold-seekers needed protection from hostile Indians, so Fort Davis was built to guard the route west. Including both ruins and restorations, Fort Davis National Historical Site presents a superb example of frontier forts of the eighteen hundreds.

The town of the same name grew up around the fort. In the town of Fort Davis is the historic Hotel Limpia, built around 1912, where you can still stay, eat, and enjoy the rocking chairs on the porch. There are also a number of other places that will welcome you warmly.

Just outside of town are the Chihuahuan Desert Visitor Center and Davis Mountains State Park. Both are popular for their camping, hiking, picnicking, and restroom facilities. The Desert Visitor Center is a scientific research and education facility with signs along the trails pointing out geologic formations and interesting facts about the plants and animals. The park also has a multilevel pueblo style hotel called Indian Lodge. Either place is well worth the time to stop.

The road leaving Fort Davis to the south starts out relatively calmly. The long hills descend into the valley, where the temperature is noticeably warmer. The long curves require a lot of lean time, which makes them even more thrilling. Hills and curves keep coming, one after another, making this stretch of the ride worth any trouble you may have had to get here.

Huge boulders dot the roadsides and the mountainsides. If there has been any severe weather recently, heed the "Watch for Falling Rocks" signs. Some might still be scattered on the roadway. Fortunately, there is very little traffic here. You are probably as likely to see another bike as you are to see a car. You will also see a lot of litter barrels, in an effort to keep this beautiful part of Texas clean and trash-free.

About twenty-five miles from Fort Davis is the town of Alpine, "Home of the Last Frontier," with a population just under 6,000. Alpine, a small, neat town, is also the home of Sul Ross University. At the second blinking red light, turn left to stay on TX 118. Then turn right at the next blinker, cross the railroad track, pass the stadium, and head out on the open road again. Study Butte is eighty miles ahead.

Alpine to Study Butte

Be sure your tank is full and you have replenished your provisions before you set out from Alpine. There are no towns for the next eighty miles. There is no place to stop for food or fuel. All you will have is what you take with you.

Almost immediately you are in the Wild West again, with very few signs of civilization other than the paved two-lane road with a small shoulder and highway signs pointing out major mountain peaks in the distance. A few houses are scattered away from the road, but, otherwise, there are very few signs of human habitation.

The landscape south of Alpine is not as rugged as it is north of town, so you can get on a bit more speed than before. The curves are still plentiful, even if they are not as harrowing as the first leg of the ride. Warning and speed signs appear whenever a wicked corkscrew or a series of sharp curves is coming. Get ready for fun because there are stretches of really good leaning. In the distance you can see the roadway winding up the hills ahead.

"This is the kind of riding I like," one biker said. "Relaxed, great views. You can really enjoy it all here."

At the beginning of this ride, the land was mountainous with green vegetation. Before long you will notice that the region has become a true desert. Here it is dry, averaging ten inches of rainfall a year or less, and definitely different from farther north. The closer you get to Study Butte, the rockier and more rugged the landscape becomes. During the flat stretches where the mountains tower in the distance, roadside signs point out their elevations. There are more and more curves and corkscrew turns. At one point mountains rise on the left of the road, and canyons plunge on the right.

Study Butte marks the end of this ride. At this point, either stop for the night, continue with the Rio Grande ride to Presidio, or proceed to

Big Bend. Whatever you decide to do, top off your fuel tank, because this will be your last chance for a while.

Highlights Along the Way

McDonald Observatory at Mount Locke. Features the Hobby-Eberly Telescope, the third largest telescope in the world. The site was selected for the observatory because of clear air, high percentage of cloudless nights, distance from artificial ground lights and dust and radiation-filtering growths of natural vegetation. Visitor Center, guided and self-guided tours. Night and day programs. 432/426-3263, www.mcdonaldobservatory.org.

Fort Davis. The town surrounding the fort. Restored and new buildings offer a glimpse into the West Texas of the 1800s. Food, lodging, and services. www.fortdavis.com.

Hotel Limpia. A restored country inn, c. 1912, known for the rattan rockers on the sun porch as well as its dining room. 100 Main St. 800/662-5517 or 432/426-3237, www.hotellimpia.com.

Fort Davis National Historic Site. Established in the mid 1800s to protect pioneers, wagon trains, mail, and gold seekers venturing west, the fort housed up to 12 companies of cavalry and infantry, many of them black "buffalo soldiers." Today it is a superb example of frontier forts, including both ruins and restored areas, a museum, and vivid interpretive re-creations. On the north side of town. 432/426-3224, www.nps.gov/foda.

Chihuahuan Desert Visitor Center. A natural area owned and managed by the Chihuahuan Desert Research Institute, includes an arboretum of plants native to this desert region, hiking trails with signs pointing out geologic formations etc., cactus greenhouse, and more. On TX 118, 3.5 miles south of Fort Davis. 432/364-2499, www.cdri.org.

Davis Mountains State Park. Almost two thousand acres in a sloping basin in the Davis Mountains. Interpretive center, camping, picnicking, dining room, hiking. On TX 118, 6 miles west of Fort Davis on Park Road 3. 800/792-1112, www.tpwd.state.tx.us/park/davis.

Indian Lodge. A full service hotel built in the 1930s to resemble southwestern Indian pueblos. 432/426-3254, www.tpwd.state.tx.us/park/indian. Located in the park.

Alpine. Texas Main Street city with historic downtown district, home of Sul Ross University. Food, fuel, and lodging. www.alpinetexas.com.

Study Butte. A mercury mining town that faded when the mines were no longer profitable, it has been revived by tourism in recent years. Limited facilities.

Big Bend Motor Inn, Hwy 118, 800/848-2363, www.ghosttowntexas.com/ghosttown.htm. Tracy's Cafe at gas station next to the motel, 432/371-2888.

Ride 2: Ride the Rio Grande
The Thrilling River Road

Some rides are thrilling, some downright adventurous and dangerous. Some have gentle curves, others have back-to-back corkscrews. Some go through populated areas, while others trek through ghost towns and deserted ruins.

This ride has the longest stretch with the most curves through the most barren terrain with the fewest people of any ride in this book. It is the most desolate, the most adventurous, and the most memorable. Everyone wants to do this ride once, but then may never repeat it. The ride is sixty-seven miles of pure riding ecstasy or pure terror. Only seasoned, experienced bikers with no fear need attempt this road.

Ride the Rio Grande follows the River Road along the meanderings of the Rio Grande. On one side of the river is the United States and on the other side is Mexico. Both sides feature rough, beautiful terrain. This is the sort of landscape that makes you want to transform your bike into a sure-footed mountain goat so you can wander everywhere up and down the rocks and canyons.

Before departing Study Butte for Presidio, be sure that your fuel tank is full, your cell phone is working, and that you have plenty of water, snacks, and anything else you might need packed in your saddlebags. After the ghost towns of Terlingua and then Lajitas at the beginning of the ride, there is nothing in the way of provisions until Presidio.

Getting Started: Study Butte to Presidio

The first indication that this is a worthy ride is the sign posted even before leaving Study Butte: "15% grade ahead, steep hills for 30 miles." You have been officially warned of what's ahead. If steep grades are not your kind of riding, now is the time to turn around and abort the mission. The rugged hills, steep grades, and roller-coaster switchbacks challenge even the most experienced riders. This road takes skill and stamina, not to mention an iron constitution. If this is your wildest fantasy, then you are about to enter a state of total euphoria.

On the way out of Study Butte, hills stretch ahead like rumpled ribbons. The next incline begins before the last ends, each rippling higher than the one before. Rugged rocks climb towards the sky from the roadside, letting you know this is a ride of a lifetime. Adventure awaits.

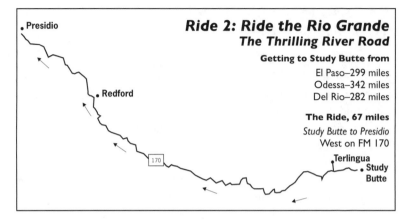

Just five miles down the road is the revived ghost town of Terlingua. Once a boisterous mining town of 2,000, it fell into ruins when the cinnabar—or mercury ore—mines closed in the 1940s. Its revival began with notoriety among chili-heads when Wick Fowler began chili cook-offs here in the 1960s. Now the ruins of the old town provide basic tourist attractions for the new but old-looking construction going on here.

Once you ride the River Road, you will also know why bikers gather here every year for a rally. Getting here might be a trial, but once you do, the challenge is worth the effort.

The rugged two-lane road passes through some low water spots that might pose a problem if there has been rain, but, considering how much rain falls here in the desert, the likelihood is slim. The double corkscrew curves through the wild, barren country start coming one after another almost as soon as you get down the first hill past Terlingua. The hills crest like a monster roller coaster, climbing steeply to the top and culminating in an unbelievable view of God's country. Then the coaster begins again with a steep decline and another ascent to the top.

Without even trying, you'll find yourself schussing down the hills, gaining momentum to scoot up the next one. Control your speed, or you may find yourself airborne as you crest the peaks. With no railing on the sides of the roads, there is no margin of error on the landing strip.

Lajitas, thirteen miles down the road from Terlingua, is a developing area being constructed to look like an old-time West Texas town. Motels, condominiums, a restaurant and saloon, and even an airport are being built. Lajitas claims Clay Henry, a beer-drinking goat, as its mayor.

As you continue on the River Road, notice a sign reminding riders of the 15 percent grade ahead for the next thirteen miles. By now you understand the warning. You also know the Department of Transportation is not joshing when it says, "Steep Grade" or slow speeds around curves. The biggest thrills are yet to come.

For the fifty miles after Lajitas, FM 170 follows the mighty Rio Grande. This strip of FM 170, completed in 1961, is known as the River Road for obvious reasons. This far upstream the Rio Grande is not the wide boundary between the United States and Mexico that it is closer to the Gulf of Mexico. Here the narrow river is a powerful water force that cuts through towering layers of rock, even though it might seem like a benign, meandering stream in places.

Big Bend Ranch State Park begins just past Lajitas. With 300,000 acres, this park exceeds the size of all other Texas state parks combined. The park, a natural area, limits the number of visitors. Park roads are gravel, not the best surface for a bike, so you may choose to stay on the main road. This route runs beside the protected area, assuring future generations of Texans that this adventure ride will still be here for them to enjoy.

The segment of FM 170 by the Rio Grande is one of the few stretches along the border that does not have a large, visible Border Patrol presence. With the tall cliffs on the Mexican side and the rugged

An old adobe building continues crumbling in the ghost town of Terlingua..

LARRY BURMEIER

The Rio Grande rambles between the United States and Mexico below the River Road.

terrain on the American side, crossing the river here, even though it is fairly narrow, is extremely difficult.

You need to ride fairly slowly as you reach the peak of each hill so you can appreciate the spectacular views that envelop you. The tall, rocky mountains, adventurous sharp turns, and magnificent desert scenery make even the hardiest soul wonder about the Universe. This is mountain riding at its most awe-inspiring.

The left side of the road goes down to the Rio Grande. As the river twists and turns, it comes in and out of sight. The road also dips and turns and climbs, just like its river namesake. A good place to stop to enjoy the scenery is at a roadside rest area about twelve miles outside of Lajitas. Teepees form shelters over picnic tables, adding to the rugged, historic atmosphere of the area. A jackalope running across the landscape would seem perfectly natural in this setting. You almost expect to have to dodge one.

When you look across the mighty Rio Grande, you see a vision of what Mexico and the entire region must have looked like to the early Spanish explorers. In the middle of all the scenic grandeur, you also begin to gain real respect for the road builders. The next five miles were among the toughest of the entire route to build. At one point the grade really is 15 percent the maximum on any regularly traveled Texas highway. A short stretch on Spur 78 to the McDonald Observatory is a bit steeper, but that is not considered a "regularly traveled route."

At the end of approximately thirty miles of steep grades, the road becomes relatively flat and straight, but not for long. There are still dips, one after another, and lots of corkscrew and regular twisting curves.

The speed limit for the sixteen miles between Redford, a retail center for the farms and ranches in the area, and Presidio is 50 mph, an increase over the fluctuating speed limits of the preceding fifty miles. The road is straighter, although it still curves sharply with double corkscrews followed by more double corkscrews with even lower speed limits. Along the road are fenced pastures and even some irrigated farmlands. Scattered houses and RV parks start popping up as Presidio draws near.

Just east of Presidio is Fort Leaton State Historic Site. Originally it was a private fort and trading post established by Ben Leaton, who, if legend supplies any truth, managed to make enemies of almost everyone, Indians and Anglos alike. Rumors claim that he was also a scalp hunter. No wonder no one liked him. Today the adobe fortress has a museum, picnicking, and a variety of special programs.

You will agree with the sign that welcomes you as you enter Presidio. It says: "Presidio – Welcome to the Real Frontier."

Highlights Along the Way

Terlingua: Once a mining ghost town, Terlingua is now the destination of tourists, Big Bend adventurers, bikers, chili-heads. www.ghosttowntexas.com
    Chisos Mining Company Motel. 432/371-2254. www.cmcm.cc.
    Starlight Theatre. Abandoned movie theater converted to a bar and eatery. Live music on weekends. 432/371-2326, www.ghosttown.com/ghosttown. htm.

Lajitas: A revived town that is experiencing a new round of development. 877/525-4827, www.lajitas.com; Clay Henry, beer-drinking goat and mayor of Lajitas, www.clayhenry.com.

Barton Warnock Environmental Education Center and **Big Bend Ranch State Park Visitors Center.** Bilingual exhibits on the archeological, historical, and natural history of the Big Bend region and botanical gardens of plants in the Chihuahuan Desert. Immediately east of Lajitas on FM 170. www.tpwd.state.tx.us/park/barton/barton.htm.

Big Bend Ranch State Park. The largest state park in Texas is maintained as a natural area with limited visitor facilities. Gravel roads and hiking trails, outstanding geological formations. Overnight facilities at Sauceda, the old ranch headquarters, are only reached only by a 25-mile gravel road. Camping in designated primitive campsites. 915/229-3416, www.tpwd.state.tx.us/park/bigbend.

Fort Leaton State Historic Site. This private fort and trading post was established in the mid-1800s by Ben Leaton, the first Anglo-American settler in the area. The restored fort has a museum, picnic tables, and family cemetery. 432/229-3613, ww.tpwd.state.tx.us/park/fortleat.

Ride 3: Desert to Springs
Presidio to Balmorhea

You have just completed the Ride the Rio Grande along the River Road, you are already in Presidio, and now you are ready to begin the last leg of the Wild West Adventure Circuit.

On the other hand, this last segment of the journey is another route south from the stretch of I-10 from San Antonio West to El Paso. Since this route is a bit calmer than the Touching Heaven ride from Kent south to Study Butte, this ride may be more to your liking to get you started. Then you can finish up the tour with the more adventurous Touching Heaven ride. There is no such thing as the wrong order to do these three rides, just different preferences.

Take a break in Presidio after coming off the River Road before heading out straight north on this next run of almost 120 miles. With a population of a little more than 4,100, Presidio can provide the fuel and services you need before embarking on your way back. Of course this ride has plenty of good road to do on its own, even without any of the other segments of the Big Bend rides.

This ride extends through some interesting areas, starting with Presidio. Cross the border here to go into Ojinaga for a bit of real Mexican culture. Eighteen miles up the road is Shafter, another ghost town. It was the location for the desolate scenes in the 1968 film "The Andromeda Strain," one of Michael Crichton's early works.

Forty-three miles past Shafter is Marfa, home of the mysterious Marfa lights and other wonders. Balmorhea, about the only place to scuba dive in the desert, is a true oasis, fed by a natural spring that irrigates farms for miles around. In between these interesting stops are miles and miles of beautiful scenery and great riding.

Getting Started: Presidio to Marfa

Presidio seems like an oasis in the middle of the desert because of the palm trees growing in a straight line along US 67. The shops, restaurants, and banks cater to the needs of people crossing the border, so you can be assured of getting some authentic Mexican food.

After fueling yourself and your bike, head north on US 67 towards Marfa. The two-lanes-plus-shoulder road is basically straight, with some gentle curves and hills over long slopes. The altitude increases gradually; you may not even realize it until you feel your ears clog and then pop. The road has more curves and gets steeper the higher into the mountains you ride. This means that the road becomes even better for riding the farther up you climb.

A corkscrew curve with a speed limit of 60 mph alerts you of fun ahead, not warning you of a dangerous ride with a speed of 15 mph as you saw on FM 170. Both types are good, but these gentler, faster curves are not quite as intimidating nor potentially as dangerous.

The arid, rocky surroundings envelop you in a panorama of West Texas landscape. Blue and purple mountains break the horizon in the distance. You might see vultures circling overhead marking the position of something freshly dead, maybe highway road kill or perhaps something in one of the pastures on either side of the road.

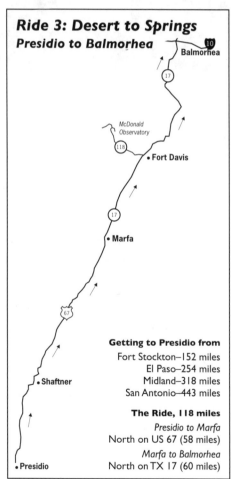

Ride 3: Desert to Springs
Presidio to Balmorhea

Balmorhea

17

McDonald
Observatory

118

• Fort Davis

17

• Marfa

67

Getting to Presidio from
Fort Stockton–152 miles
El Paso–254 miles
Midland–318 miles
San Antonio–443 miles

• Shaftner

The Ride, 118 miles
Presidio to Marfa
North on US 67 (58 miles)
Marfa to Balmorhea
North on TX 17 (60 miles)

• Presidio

Spectacular vistas unfold along twisting US 67 north of Presidio.

Signs point out such places of interest as Shafter, a ghost town. You can almost feel the spirits of souls past lurking in the shadows of Shafter's old church, cemetery, and historical marker. Evidence has been found to indicate that farmers lived here as long ago as 1500 BC, making this the oldest continually cultivated land in the entire United States. But when the silver boom went bust, the people left.

Just a bit farther on, a sign points out a mountaintop shaped like the profile of Lincoln. Right after Honest Abe you will ride another 50 mph corkscrew turn. Another sign points out Chianti Peak, on your left, more than 7,700 feet high.

Looking ahead at the zigzagging road, and knowing that before long that is exactly where you will be riding, creates anticipation for what's coming up. The farther north the road goes, the more rounded the mountaintops become, and the grassier and less rocky the surrounding areas are. The rugged landscape now sports peaks and rocks not as sharp and craggy as on the River Road. Fences run alongside the road, but that does not mean there will be any cattle visible from the road. Desert land takes a lot of acreage to support a herd, and they may be off in the "back forty" or elsewhere.

US 67 is part of the Texas Mountain Trail, and the hills continue to roller coaster up and down. You may feel the increase in altitude in your ears. Although there are only two lanes, an occasional extra passing lane helps when there is slow traffic.

Everyone has heard of the famous Marfa lights. They were first reported in 1883 and have been mystifying mortals ever since. To see them, go nine miles east of the city on US 90. An historical marker marks the spot. If you decide to stay over for a viewing, stop at any of the many places to rest your head in this picturesque town of a little over two thousand residents. The Marfa Book Co. /Coffee & Wine Bar serves refreshments, whatever your pleasure may happen to be.

Even though most bikers are not also golfers, the highest golf course in Texas is located here in Marfa at an altitude of almost a mile.

Marfa to Balmorhea

When you depart Marfa, you pass a huge complex of greenhouses near the airport. Your veggies might come from here.

TX 17 out of Marfa is a smooth two-lane road with shoulder. The vegetation along the side gets grassier, with fewer cactus and scrubby shrubs than to the south. There are more and longer straightaways mixed in with gentle hills. There may even be a few more trucks and cars. Once you have ridden without meeting another vehicle for fifteen minutes or more at a time, seeing one every few minutes seems to be pretty often.

The glittery domes of the McDonald Observatory reflecting sunlight into the desolate surroundings are incongruous with the rugged landscape. But the high altitude, clean air, and lack of ground light make this the ideal location for searching the heavens, which is why a consortium of five universities built it here in the first place. The steep curve up to the 6,791-foot peak of Mount Locke, where the largest telescope is located, is a riding adventure in itself, even if you have no interest in stargazing.

Fort Davis, on the other side of the observatory, is another fun place chock full of history. For an example of a frontier fort from the gold-rush era of Western expansion, go to the Fort Davis National Historical Site. Fort Davis has a number of good places to eat and sleep, including the historic Hotel Limpia, Butterfield Inn, and Pop's Grill, all on TX 118 through town.

At Fort Davis go north (right) to stay on TX 17 towards Balmorhea. The curves and hills leaving Fort Davis are not as treacherous and dangerous as before. This fun route lessens the underlying element of potential danger of earlier roads.

The two lanes plus shoulder go around the mountains rather than over them. The twists and curves, corkscrews and switchbacks keep coming one after another. You feel like you are going to bounce directly into a stone wall as you come around one curve marked with a 40 mph sign. But then the road curves in the nick of time.

The Wild Rose Pass goes between the mountains about ten miles outside Fort Davis. Each time you come around one of the gentle curves the view changes for the better. Signs tell of upcoming curves, and the posted speed limit gives clues as to their severity. The long hills and curves gradually decrease in altitude and are interspersed with stretches of exhilarating twists and turns.

The pastures get grassier as you ride toward the north. Occasionally you will even see an isolated house off in the distance. You can see mountains in the foreground as well as in the distance, making the scenery as intriguing as the riding.

At I-10, stay on TX 17 to the right. The source of the historic San Solomon Springs, a watering hole for buffalo, Indians, and pioneers, is located in Balmorhea State Park. Today the springs supply irrigation needs of the area as well as one of the largest man-made pools in the United States. There are very few other places in the world where it is possible for you to scuba dive in the desert.

Either stay in Balmorhea or get on I-10 to travel to other locales. If you have combined this ride with the Touching Heaven Ride and the Ride the Rio Grande, you have proven yourself to be a dedicated biker and have experienced some of the best, most scenic, and most desolate roads in the entire state.

Highlights Along the Way

Presidio. The early Spanish settlement was protected by a fort or presidio, hence its name. Gateway to Ojinaga, Mexico. http://presidiotex.com.

El Patio Cafe. Mexican food including tacos, fajitas, breakfast, and ice cream. Reilly Street in downtown Presidio, 432/229-4409.

Three Palms Inn. North Business 67, 432/229-3211.

Presidio La Siesta Motel. North Business 67 near downtown, 432/229-3611.

Shafter. Riding is tricky on a gravel main street to see the old church, cemetery and historical marker, plus spirits from the past. Off US 67 south of Marfa.

Marfa. Established as a railroad water stop, today Marfa enjoys popularity with hunters and other tourists, especially those interested in viewing the mysterious Marfa Lights. http://marfatx.com.

Marfa Book Co./Coffee & Wine Bar offers reads and drinks. 105 S. Highland St. 432/729-3906, http://marfabookco.com.

Marfa Lights Viewing Center features a viewing deck, restrooms, and information about the lights and local area. 8 miles east of Marfa on US 67/90. http://marfatx.com/b_lights.asp.

Riata Inn. Highway 90 East. 432/729-3800, www.marfatx.com/c_food.asp.

Borunda's Bar and Grill. Mexican food, hamburgers, pool tables. 113 S. Russell St. 432/729-8163, www.marfatx.com/c_food.asp.

Carmen's Cafe. Mexican dishes, burgers, and sandwiches. 317 E. San Antonio St. 432/729-3429, www.marfatx.com/.c_food.asp.

McDonald Observatory at Mount Locke. See Ride 1.

Fort Davis. The town surrounding Fort Davis, where restored and new buildings offer a glimpse into the West Texas of the 1800s. Food, lodging, services. www.fortdavis.com.

Fort Davis National Historical Site. Established in the mid-1800s to protect pioneers, wagon trains, mail, and gold seekers venturing west, the fort housed up to twelve companies of cavalry and infantry, many of them black "buffalo soldiers." This superb example of a frontier fort includes both ruins and restored areas, a museum, and vivid interpretive recreations. On the north side of town on TX 118. 432/426-3224, www.nps.gov/foda.

Balmorhea State Park. The San Solomon Springs feed a huge 62,000 square foot pool, one of the largest in the nation. Swimming and scuba diving in the pool. Motel, camping rest rooms with hot showers, picnic areas, and playground. 432/375-2370, www.tpwd.tx.us/park/balmorhe.

Ride 4: A Taste of Heaven
Adventurous Riding in the Wild West

Unexpectedly, you find yourself with a few extra days, a gift of time that suddenly materialized. You want adventure. You want great riding. You want to get away from your usual trails and experience something new and exciting. But you don't want to do an unofficial iron butt run. Where to ride?

There is only one answer to that question.

Take off for West Texas.

No matter where you're from, you will travel a long way to the beginning of the ride. In spite of all your effort, once you have made this

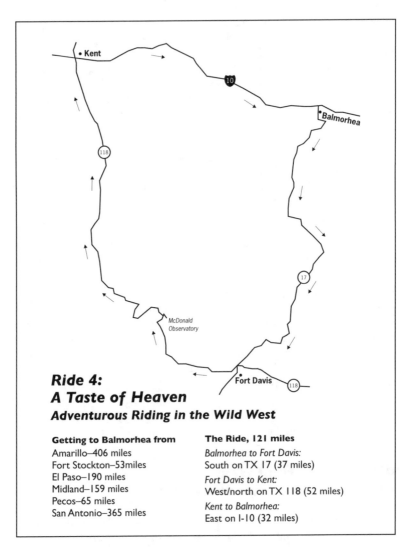

Ride 4:
A Taste of Heaven
Adventurous Riding in the Wild West

Getting to Balmorhea from
Amarillo—406 miles
Fort Stockton—53miles
El Paso—190 miles
Midland—159 miles
Pecos—65 miles
San Antonio—365 miles

The Ride, 121 miles
Balmorhea to Fort Davis:
South on TX 17 (37 miles)
Fort Davis to Kent:
West/north on TX 118 (52 miles)
Kent to Balmorhea:
East on I-10 (32 miles)

ride you will agree it is worth the effort, especially if you take the scenic state highways to get here. The abbreviated ride gives you a taste of the heavenly riding in West Texas's Big Bend region in a relatively short period of time.

This ride takes the best of the West Texas rides and combines them into one shorter yet still challenging route. Start in Balmorhea, loop down to Fort Davis, and circle by the McDonald Observatory on the way to Kent. You'll see a sign for the Scenic Route on TX 166. This course loops from just south of Fort Davis around and through the Davis Mountains and connects with TX 118 on the way to Kent. Try this route for more heavenly riding. However, don't miss the trek up to the observatory even if stargazing is not your passion. The riding will make you glad you did.

No matter which loop you choose, you will experience great, adventurous riding that will take you past some of the most spectacular views in the state. As with all the rides that go through isolated areas, be sure you let someone know your itinerary. Carry plenty of water, fuel and food, and dress in layers that you can peel as the temperatures change. Take along your cell, even though it may not work in places, and wear protection.

After this taste of heavenly riding, you will take a solemn vow to return so you can explore more of this celestial region.

Getting Started: Balmorhea to Fort Davis

If you dream of riding on empty roads through rugged territory, then this is the ride for you. Getting to Balmorhea on I-10 from almost any place you are coming from will be an adventure. But don't let the idea of riding a typical divided interstate highway lull you into complacency. Even though the road flattens a lot of the mountains and curves, you'll still enjoy getting to the launching pad for this ride. There won't be a lot of traffic, but there may be some. After all, I-10 is one of the main east-west thoroughfares across the state. Looking into the distance you'll feel the isolation and harshness of the landscape. Even before getting to the starting point of the ride you'll get the idea that the roads here are absolutely nothing like the flat, straight roads in the Gulf Coast plains.

If you are coming from the east heading west, take a left on TX 17 toward the south off I-10 toward Fort Davis. Immediately the riding changes. Now you can get the full sensation of the hills, feel the curves, and almost caress the road with your bike. The riding is several notches above the caliber of riding on the interstate, but nothing at all like what you will be experiencing later. This soft sample of what is coming up will whet your appetite for the thrills ahead.

As you head south on TX 17, the grassy roadside pastures are filled with scrubby shrubs and rocks. The fenced pastures may appear to be vacant, but that is only because the livestock are munching elsewhere on the spread. The individual ranches around here are bigger than some small nations because huge acreage is needed to support the herds.

The farther south you travel, the more mountainous the terrain becomes. The road starts with long hills, the next one starting before the last one has ended and gradually reaching higher and higher altitudes. Ribbons of long, gentle curves alternate with stretches of serious twists and turns. Reduced speed limit signs indicate the severity of the road ahead. The lower the posted miles per hour, the sharper or twistier the curves. An occasional house far off the side of the road reminds you that this is not an abandoned world. Although threats from indigenous peoples no longer exit, you can easily imagine the possibility. Shadows of native scouts on the crests of high mesas seem almost real.

Each time you go around a curve the view gets better than the one before. As one curve follows another, the fantastic vistas keep coming in seemingly endless succession. Fortunately, there are frequent picnic stops so you can pull off to the side and gaze in amazement at the landscape. In the distance you'll see towering mountains and mesas reaching towards the sky. The blues above seem bluer here and the heavens seem to wrap around the earth for even more than the 180 degrees that your brain tells you is the maximum possible. Even the clouds appear bolder and fuller than any you have ever seen.

This gorgeous riding extends for 37 miles along a two-lane road all the way to Fort Davis.

Fort Davis to Kent

Now the real fun begins. Up to this point the ride has merely been a warm-up for what is to come. Just before coming to the Fort Davis National Historical Site, you passed the intersection of TX 17 with TX 118. To continue this ride, go west—right if you are coming from Balmorhea, left if you stopped in Fort Davis. Head into the Davis Mountains State Park. Your biker buddies who have ridden the West Texas roads have told tall tales about this area. Now you will see they weren't lies; the stories are all true.

The craggy mountains are steeper and rockier than before. Tall mesas in the distance appear close because of the sheer volume of stone and earth rising up from below. The flat tops are bordered by upright boulders that appear to be guarding the passageway below. You can see the zigzags in the road's many twists and turns before you actually get there. Signs giving lower speed limits warn of the severity of the curves. After a while, a 50 mph curve will seem like a bit of nothing after riding others at 25 or 30 mph.

Even if you have no interest in astronomy, take Spur 77 to the McDonald Observatory. Here are some of the steepest grades in the entire state. Add in hairpin turns, a cattle guard, and steep drop-offs on the side of the road and you are in for an adventure. Here you will need to use your gears, especially when you leave the area and take the sharp descents while going around the curves. The speed limit ranges from 15 to 30 mph, which gives you an idea of the type of riding you're dealing with here. At an altitude of about 6,790 feet at the top, your ears may clog and then pop on the way down.

Take it easy on these roads. Don't think you are on a "Riding for Dummies" course. Caution and common sense are mandatory here, even for experienced riders. Also watch out for cyclists here. Some folks work too hard for their fun.

After making your way up and back down the mountain, retrace your path to TX 118 and continue north towards Kent. If you thought the trek on TX 17 from Balmorhea to Kent was good riding, this next stretch will seem like ecstasy. The normal posted speed limit is 75 mph, higher than anywhere else in the state. The folks here know that is a reasonable speed. When a sign says something less, trust that the speed is reasonable.

The narrow two-lane road features sharp curves that frequently make even the posted speed limit seem a bit high. Double yellow stripes remind you not to pass, but, then, there probably won't be anything to pass, except for your riding buddies. Riding here is not for novices or weak stomachs.

The narrow road has an even narrower shoulder. Fortunately, there are some places to pull off to the side if you need or want to take a break or check out a problem. Otherwise, most of the time, the side of the road just does not have room to stop safely. Signs occasionally warn of potential flash flooding. Sudden rains don't happen often, but when they do, beware.

The panoramic views of the mountains are the visions of your dreams. The hills, curves, and long ascents up the mountains and then down are what riding fantasies are made of. The road slips in and out of valleys with long straightaways between climbing up and around another mountain. Here you'll pass by more huge ranches where, once again, you may or may not see anything behind the fences.

If you have time to notice, you'll see that many fence posts here are the old-fashioned kind, hearty sticks of different sizes and shapes, with barbed wire strung from one to the next. You won't see fencing like this in the Lakes and Prairie rides when you ride by manicured horse farms.

Kent to Balmorhea

About thirty-nine miles after leaving the McDonald Observatory you will come to the end of the adventure ride at Kent. Turn east (right) on I-10 and head back towards Balmorhea. You have experienced a taste of heavenly West Texas.

Highlights Along the Way

See Ride 1 (Touching Heaven) and Ride 2 (Desert to Springs) for information on locations passed on this ride.

Prairies and Lakes

No one will ever confuse a leather-clad twenty-first century Texas biker with a nineteenth-century English poet. But once you have been in the Texas Lake District in the northern part of the state, you will understand why the Brits wax so eloquently about the beauty of nature on their tours of the English countryside. Being surrounded by the beauty of lakes and forests stirs the soul. This area renews your spirit.

The Texas Prairies and Lakes region has fantastic riding for experts and novices alike. Some rides are gentle, but they are all awe-inspiring because of the restorative properties of being surrounded by trees, water, and gorgeous rural countryside.

In spite of the pastoral setting, much of this area was a hotbed of discontent. Parts of the Texas Independence Trail, which focuses on the fight for freedom from Mexico, are here. Some rides go to places you may have heard about only in seventh grade Texas history, assuming you paid more attention than most other kids in the class. Today these areas celebrate their illustrious past in festivals and in carefully preserving buildings and remnants of the friendly atmosphere of days gone by.

These lakes, unlike those in the Lake District of England, have the distinction of being mostly man-made. They are a welcome by-product of dams erected for flood control. Regardless of the mundane reason for their creation, the resulting network of beautiful lakes provides solace as well as recreational activities to everyone who visits.

The Prairies and Lakes area provide pure riding bliss. When you want to stop, you can either learn something at a historical site or zone out in deep, or shallow, contemplation in one of the idyllic locations.

Ride 5: The Independence Ride
Brenham, Burton, Independence, Washington-On-The-Brazos

Stephen F. Austin's original 300 families knew a good place when they saw one. A number of the first settlers stopped in what is now Washington County. This area abounds with the history that led to the signing of the Texas Declaration of Independence and creation of the independent Republic of Texas. Numerous points of interest exist in Washington County, highlighted by 133 historical markers and probably at least another hundred or so other reasons to stop. This relatively short ride allows time for you to stop at places that interest you. You have much to choose from. But most of all, enjoy your independence as you take the curves and hills of this segment of the Texas Independence Trail.

This ride also follows portions of the Texas Bluebonnet Trail. If you ride this route in the spring, you will be rewarded with some of the best wildflower sightings in the state. You'll pass fields of blue that look like the ocean from the great masses of our state flower, the bluebonnet. Unfortunately, other folks are also on the trail, flower gawking, and that can make this road a bit crowded for an independent rider. But don't let the threat of crowds deter you. Fortunately, whenever you go, the riding is great, and even without bluebonnets, the scenery and riding are worth the trip.

Washington County boasts at least one festival every month of the year, except August. Time your ride right and you can join in the fun or avoid the revelry entirely.

In fact, there are more interesting places to stop along this route than other rides of the same distance in this book. Stop at those that interest you, but if you stop at them all on one trip you won't finish this short ride until sometime next Thursday, at the earliest. Stop at enough so you'll be fresh enough to enjoy the full effect of the gentle hills and curves and the especially twisty ones that switch back and forth. Then come back, do the ride again, and hit those you missed the first time.

Families especially enjoy this ride because something is sure to interest everyone. The educational stops are great for the kids, and the riding is fun without being too strenuous for those with less experience. You can head back to your starting point at several places along the route. So if you or someone in your group gets tuckered out and needs to quit the ride, no problem. As always, have fun, ride safe, and do not try to break any endurance records.

Getting Started: Brenham to Burton

One good way to start this ride is with a detour to the Blue Bell Creameries in Brenham. Every true Texan, native or not, knows that the

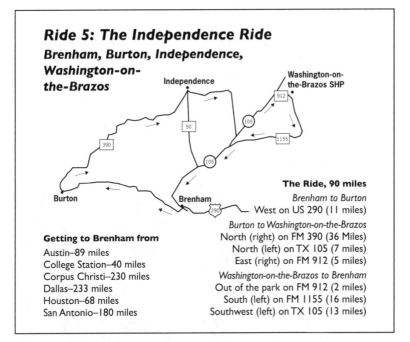

Ride 5: The Independence Ride
Brenham, Burton, Independence, Washington-on-the-Brazos

Independence

Washington-on-the-Brazos SHP

The Ride, 90 miles

Brenham to Burton
West on US 290 (11 miles)

Burton to Washington-on-the-Brazos
North (right) on FM 390 (36 Miles)
North (left) on TX 105 (7 miles)
East (right) on FM 912 (5 miles)

Washington-on-the-Brazos to Brenham
Out of the park on FM 912 (2 miles)
South (left) on FM 1155 (16 miles)
Southwest (left) on TX 105 (13 miles)

Getting to Brenham from

Austin–89 miles
College Station–40 miles
Corpus Christi–230 miles
Dallas–233 miles
Houston–68 miles
San Antonio–180 miles

ice cream made in Brenham is the gold standard in the state. Take a tour unless you are itching to get on the road. Then, just stop for a scoop. Of course, Blue Bell will still be here when you return so you can always get some more of the cold stuff when you get back.

If you want something stronger, take a jaunt south on TX 36 from Brenham to Salem Road and go about another mile and a half to FM 3456. Here you will find the Pleasant Hill Winery that offers tours, tastings, and a fascinating collection of corkscrews and vintage televisions and radios.

Or do what you started out to do and continue on US 290 towards Burton. This easy ride begins with long rolling hills. You can enjoy the pleasant scenery and appreciate the calm, fun riding. Feel the road and commune with your bike.

As you approach Burton, you'll see the sign to the Burton Cotton Gin and Museum. Here you will not find your typical historic exhibits with spinning wheels and open-fire cooking. This one instead emphasizes more mechanical things, such as the restored cotton gin and old cars.

Burton to Independence

When you get to Burton, take a sharp right onto FM 390. This first turn is a harbinger of the kind of riding you are about to enjoy. From here on, you will experience lots of sharp turns, 90-degree curves, corkscrews and switchbacks, alternating with gentle curves and hills and pleasantly windy roads. While you are on one of the easy stretches of two-lane country road, relax and enjoy, because a more challenging stretch will follow soon.

You will ride by ranch land with pastures of cattle, fields of hay, and lots of scattered trees that give shade to the livestock and make a picturesque view for everyone to enjoy. You'll see the sign to Lake Somerville off to your left. You can enjoy the lake, camping, and hiking on over thirteen miles of trails.

This picnic site is near the original site of Baylor College's female campus, which moved to Waco.

Longpoint, at the intersection of TX 390 and FM 2679, marks the beginning of a stretch of road that consists of one curve after another. Signs warn of corkscrew turns with lower speed limits. If there has been a lot of rain, watch out for flooding and water on the road.

After passing through the community of Gay Hill, the road starts a bit straighter than before, with some calm, long rolling hills. Then the road starts curving more and the hills get a little steeper. You begin seeing more horses in the pastures; you'll even pass a cutting horse ranch that specializes in a totally different kind of horsepower than the kind you are on. Off the road in the distance you will see some huge, beautiful ranch houses. If you had that yard to mow, you wouldn't be on your bike right now.

At West Spur 390, as you approach Independence, you'll see Old Baylor Park, the campus of the original Baylor College that was eventually moved to Waco. The stone columns mark the site of the Female

College. Men attended the university on a hill to the south and across the "River Jordan." The park has a shady picnic area nestled among various early nineteenth century buildings of the school.

If you want to cut the ride short, turn right at FM 50 in Independence to go back to Brenham. Or you can continue going straight on FM 390 for more good riding. You'll pass more historic houses, ruins, and markers. If you like plants, the Antique Rose Emporium has more than just romantic old garden roses. It has herbs, a wildflower meadow, an early 1900s Victorian home, and more. Scenic East FM 390 definitely earns the scenic part of its name. Make a sharp right at the dead end. When you come to the intersection with TX 105, turn left to follow the rest of this ride. Or you can turn right to go back to Brenham.

Ride five miles on the soft curves of this two-lane country road to Washington-On-The-Brazos State Historic Site. The constitution for the Republic of Texas was adopted here. Washington-On-The-Brazos was also the first capital of the Republic of Texas. The park offers hiking trails, picnic areas, tours, and the Barrington Living History Farm. As in all state parks, bikes have to stay on the designated roadways.

Washington-On-The-Brazos to Brenham

To return to Brenham, rather than going to the park, go four miles and turn south (right) on FM 1155. If you go to the park, turn left on FM 1155 a mile after you come out of the historic area for the rest of the ride. The road passes through rolling pastures before the two lanes start to make sharp turns, some 90 degrees, and some crazy corkscrews. Like a well-endowed body, this stretch has luscious curves interspersed with calmer bits. After miles of white fences outlining pastures along the road, the fences change to black, probably marking a change in ownership of the land.

After you have been on FM 1155 for about ten miles, you'll come to an intersection. Make the sharp left turn to stay on FM 1155 and to make a detour to Chappell Hill and the Chappell Hill Historical Museum. Or continue on this ride by going straight and getting on FM 2193, which will connect with TX 105 after about three twisty miles of good riding. TX 105 is a wide two-lane highway with long curves and long hills, ideal for pleasant riding.

As you approach Brenham, you'll see the Silver Wings Ballroom on your left, a lively place to stop, especially on nights when there is a band and dancing. Or you can go straight for about two miles to get back on US 290. Unless you are in a hurry to leave, follow the signs to the historic district and enjoy the nostalgia of the town square, plus the tasty, home cooking at the Fluff Top Roll Restaurant or one of the other homey eateries.

Highlights Along the Way

Blue Bell Creameries. See the famous ice cream being made on one of the frequent tours given throughout the day. The fee includes a scoop of Blue Bell ice cream – or skip the tour and go straight to the cold stuff. FM 57 north of US 290. 800/327-8135, www.bluebell.com.

Pleasant Hill Winery. Tours on weekends, tastings, corkscrew collection, vintage televisions, radios. US 290 to TX 36 South, 1.5 miles south on Salem Rd to FM 3456. 1441 Salem Rd. 979/830-8463, www.pleasanthillwinery.com.

Burton Cotton Gin and Museum. Restored operational 1925 oil engine cotton gin. Other historic buildings include a shoe shop, warehouse, and auto shop. A Historic Mechanical Engineering Landmark, among other designations. 307 N. Main St. in Burton. 979/289-3378, www.cottonginmuseum.org.

Brenham. www.BrenhamTexas.com.

Legends Billiards & Grill. Pizza, beer, games, big-screen TV, etc. 1503 Hwy 290 East. 979/251-7665.

Tex's Bar-B-Que & Catering. Indoor dining, picnic area, take-out. 4807 Hwy. 105. 979/836-5962.

Fluff Top Roll Restaurant. Daily buffet of hearty home cooking and great rolls. 210 E. Alamo St., on historic Brenham Square. 979/836-9441.

Lake Somerville State Park. Roads and hiking trails wind through meadows and woodlands. The Nails Creek section has a sand volleyball court on the shore. Electrical and non-electrical campsites available. Nails Creek area, 979/289-2392; Birch Creek area, 979/535-7763. www.tpwd.state.tx.us/park.

Old Baylor Park. Site of the original Baylor University. Ruins of original buildings, historic homes, and one of the best places in the state to see bluebonnets in the spring. FM 390 about a mile south of Independence.

Antique Rose Emporium. Eight acres of roses, native plants, herbs, wildflowers, as well as various historic buildings. 9300 Lueckemeyer Rd. 979/836-5548, www.weAREroses.com.

Washington-On-The-Brazos State Historic Site is located on the site of the town of Washington. The complex includes a reconstruction of Independence Hall—where the Texas Declaration of Independence was signed on March 2, 1836 and the government of the nation was formed—and the Star of the Republic Museum, which provides an interesting history of the ten-year period

Burton to Independence

When you get to Burton, take a sharp right onto FM 390. This first turn is a harbinger of the kind of riding you are about to enjoy. From here on, you will experience lots of sharp turns, 90-degree curves, corkscrews and switchbacks, alternating with gentle curves and hills and pleasantly windy roads. While you are on one of the easy stretches of two-lane country road, relax and enjoy, because a more challenging stretch will follow soon.

You will ride by ranch land with pastures of cattle, fields of hay, and lots of scattered trees that give shade to the livestock and make a picturesque view for everyone to enjoy. You'll see the sign to Lake Somerville off to your left. You can enjoy the lake, camping, and hiking on over thirteen miles of trails.

This picnic site is near the original site of Baylor College's female campus, which moved to Waco.

Longpoint, at the intersection of TX 390 and FM 2679, marks the beginning of a stretch of road that consists of one curve after another. Signs warn of corkscrew turns with lower speed limits. If there has been a lot of rain, watch out for flooding and water on the road.

After passing through the community of Gay Hill, the road starts a bit straighter than before, with some calm, long rolling hills. Then the road starts curving more and the hills get a little steeper. You begin seeing more horses in the pastures; you'll even pass a cutting horse ranch that specializes in a totally different kind of horsepower than the kind you are on. Off the road in the distance you will see some huge, beautiful ranch houses. If you had that yard to mow, you wouldn't be on your bike right now.

At West Spur 390, as you approach Independence, you'll see Old Baylor Park, the campus of the original Baylor College that was eventually moved to Waco. The stone columns mark the site of the Female

College. Men atte the "River Jordan. various early ninete

If you want to c dence to go back to FM 390 for more go and markers. If you lik than just romantic old an early 1900s Victoria nitely earns the scenic p end. When you come to low the rest of this ride. (

Ride five miles on the Washington-On-The-Braz the Republic of Texas was was also the first capital of the trails, picnic areas, tours, and in all state parks, bikes have t

Washington-On-The-Bra

To return to Brenham, rath and turn south (right) on FM 1 FM 1155 a mile after you come the ride. The road passes through start to make sharp turns, some 9(Like a well-endowed body, this str with calmer bits. After miles of w. the road, the fences change to bla ownership of the land.

After you have been on FM 115 to an intersection. Make the sharp l to make a detour to Chappell Hill a Museum. Or continue on this ride by g 2193, which will connect with TX 105 good riding. TX 105 is a wide two-lane long hills, ideal for pleasant riding.

As you approach Brenham, you'll se on your left, a lively place to stop, especi

band and dancing, back on US 290. U the historic distric tasty, home cookin homey eateries.

Highlights Alon

Blue Bell Creame frequent tours give ice cream – or ski US 290. 800/327–

Pleasant Hill Wi tage televisions, r to FM 3456. 144

Burton Cotton (gin. Other histor Historic Mecha N. Main St. in I

Brenham. www Legends I Hwy 290 East Tex's Bar– Hwy. 105. 979 Fluff Top rolls. 210 E. A

Lake Somer ows and woo the shore. E 979/289-23(

Old Baylor ings, histori in the sprin

Antique R ers, as well www.weA

Washingt town of V Hall—wh 1836 and public M

when Texas was an independent nation. The Barrington Living History Farm recreates daily life on a 1850s Brazos Valley cotton farm with buildings, crops, and livestock of the period. Interpreters dressed in nineteenth century clothing perform the daily activities of the time. The park also has hiking trails, picnic areas, grills, shelters, and a conference center. As in all state parks, motorized vehicles are limited to roadways only. FM 1155 off TX 105 between Brenham and Navasota. 936/878-2214, www.birthplaceoftexas.com.

Chappell Hill Historical Museum. Permanent exhibits on the plantation economy, Civil War, Reconstruction, and two educational institutions that existed here. Church Street, Chappell Hill.

Ride 6: Dino Run
Glen Rose, Granbury, and Dinosaurs

To ride to Glen Rose means to follow in some very big footsteps. The very first sauropod tracks in the world were discovered in this area. The sauropods were plant-eating reptiles more than sixty feet long and weighing thirty tons. Their footprints are particularly well preserved in the Dinosaur Valley State Park just outside of Glen Rose. Tracks of other prehistoric reptiles are preserved in the bed of the Paluxy River that runs through these parts.

This ride detours through Cleburne State Park, one of the few places where you can actually get off your bike and rent a kayak or electric-powered boat. That form of transportation might not be as exciting as your bike, but even an iron butt needs an occasional break.

The more recent past of the nineteenth and early twentieth centuries is also preserved in the historic areas of Granbury and Glen Rose. If you come to this region on a weekend, you will see lots of your fellow motorcyclists.

Of course, bikers come here for more than just the opportunity to see fossilized dinosaur tracks and old courthouse squares. As interesting as they may be, the real thrill here is the riding. The Dino Run links together interesting stops with gently rolling hills and curves that are almost downright adventurous in places.

A word of warning: when you get off the beaten path in this area, the roads are not well marked and they can be very confusing. It is quite easy to get lost. Sometimes the paving even peters out and you'll find yourself on slippery gravel. Whatever the situation on this ride or any other, be observant and follow the route, or your fossil may be discov-

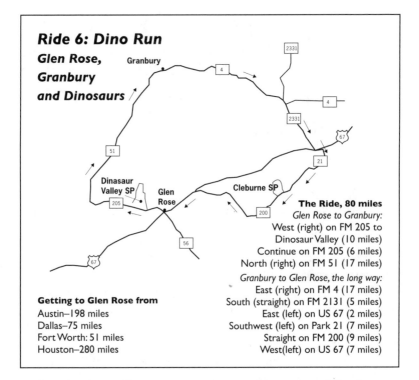

Ride 6: Dino Run

Glen Rose, Granbury and Dinosaurs

The Ride, 80 miles

Glen Rose to Granbury:
West (right) on FM 205 to
Dinosaur Valley (10 miles)
Continue on FM 205 (6 miles)
North (right) on FM 51 (17 miles)

Granbury to Glen Rose, the long way:
East (right) on FM 4 (17 miles)
South (straight) on FM 2131 (5 miles)
East (left) on US 67 (2 miles)
Southwest (left) on Park 21 (7 miles)
Straight on FM 200 (9 miles)
West (left) on US 67 (7 miles)

Getting to Glen Rose from
Austin–198 miles
Dallas–75 miles
Fort Worth: 51 miles
Houston–280 miles

ered in the next millennium somewhere in the vicinity of the dinosaur tracks.

Getting Started: Glen Rose to Granbury

Find your way to the Courthouse Square in Glen Rose to start a riding adventure that will take you back into time a few thousand years. If you are coming from the Cleburne area, follow US 67. The closer to Glen Rose you get, the better the riding gets, even on a US highway. The changes are subtle, but you realize they are occurring. Turn left at the sign pointing the way to the historic district.

The approach to old-time Glen Rose is beautiful, with tall trees along the winding Paluxy River. Quaint bed-and-breakfasts and lovely old homes welcome visitors as they come into town. The entrance to the town looks like an idyllic setting for either a romance novel or a murder mystery, depending on whether the author is a babe or a biker. Watch for cross traffic.

Unique shops and restaurants surround the courthouse square. Two Grannies' serves down home cookin' and they have a particular liking for bikers. Everyone who walks in the door gets a big bear hug from at least one of the grannies—June Thomas or Gloria Whitley. Anderson's Restaurant on the square also serves good, hearty food. Be sure to save room for homemade pie.

Leaving the square, pass Grannies and go straight on FM 56 to FM 205. The road has two lanes, a double yellow stripe down the center much of the way, and no shoulder. FM 205 crosses over US 67 about three miles before the entrance to Dinosaur Valley State Park. Sedate hills and curves come one after another on this stretch. Everyone, veterans as well as novices, enjoys riding this road. If you don't stop on this trip, make sure you come back some other time to see numerous three-toed tracks made by carnivorous dinosaurs and large, round sauropod tracks. Prepare to get wet, because the dino tracks are in and around the water.

After leaving Dinosaur Valley State Park, turn right to continue on FM 205 for a thrill-seeker stretch, with one "S" curve after another on gentle hills. The speed limit is 60 mph, but many curves are marked with lower limits. The short bits of straight stretches between the zigzags continue going up and down in hills that look like ripples of highway. There is enough terrain here to hold everyones' interest.

FM 205 dead-ends into FM 51/205. Turn right. Two miles down the two lane, no- shoulder road is the small town of Paluxy, named after the river. The yellow stripe switches from one lane to the other and then, for a while, both stripes run down the center of the road. These are the places where the road is the most fun. Beautiful North Texas rolling hills slip by. The smooth roads and curves straighten under your bike.

Follow FM 51 into Granbury. Turn left at the dead end to find your way to the courthouse square. As you enter the town you can see the courthouse clock tower rising above the trees. Use it as a beacon to historic downtown Granbury. Buildings around the square were built of locally-quarried limestone in the 1880s and '90s. In the 1970s the entire square became the first Texas site listed on the National Register of Historic Places.

The Granbury Opera House, built in 1886 and reopened in 1975, hosts plays, musicals, and melodramas throughout the year. For a different type of entertainment, go to the 1950s-vintage Brazos Drive-In, one of only twelve still in operation in Texas. Good places to eat around the square include such old favorites as the Nutshell Eatery and Bakery and the Nutt House.

Riding away from the square, leave Granbury on FM 377/4. Take a dip at the beach on Lake Granbury, if you're so inclined, or continue across the bridge over the lake and go through Acton. Go straight on FM 377 as if you are going to Fort Worth until the road dead ends. Stay on FM 4. The gravesite of Elizabeth Crockett, second wife of the famous Texas hero Davy, is located here at Texas's smallest state park.

In a few miles you'll be back in biker country. You might even see some longhorns grazing in pastures by the side of the road. Slow

Granbury's picturesque courthouse tower rises through the trees of the town square.

drivers pose one of the biggest hazards around here because some act as if they own the road. Since they probably live around here, they sort of do. Watch out for them; they won't be looking out for you.

FM 4 turns to the left at the junction with FM 2331. Stay straight to take FM 2331 back to US 67. Follow the sign that points the way to Bono. You'll pass the Stanton Branch Ranch, as well as other large landholdings, on your way back to the highway. Now you can really ride and become one with your bike. Enjoy the wind, the fresh air, and traveling along a great road.

When you get to US 67, turn left. In about a mile, turn right onto Park Road 21. This road will take you to Cleburne State Park. The ride to the park is six miles of good curves, one after another. The two-lane road has double yellow stripes and only a small shoulder. Cleburne State Park is a scenic area and wildlife refuge on the shores of Cedar Lake. The park has camping, picnicking, rest rooms, showers, and boat rentals.

When you continue on the same road after the entrance to the park, the number changes to FM 200. Stay on FM 200 and you will pass the mines of the Texas Lime Company. Then take the curves and hills through pastures and trees. You can get on a little speed, especially going down the hills. Know what you can handle, obey the speed limits, and have fun.

You might not see many other vehicles on this farm road. If you do see someone else, the chances are good it will be either another bike or some sort of farm vehicle.

When you get to the junction of FM 199/200, turn right. The two lanes will take you back to US 67. Go left to return to Glen Rose, or turn right to go towards Cleburne or Dallas.

Highlights Along the Way

Glen Rose. Information on local attractions at www.glenrosetexas.net.
  Two Grannies Down Home Cooking. Get a hug from Granny. 109 W. Barnard St. on the square. 254/897-9773.
  Anderson's Tea Room. Great pie! 102 W. Walnut St. on the square. 254/897-9421.

Dinosaur Valley State Park: One-hundred-million-year-old dinosaur tracks here. www.tpwd.state.tx.us/park.

Granbury. Information on attractions, restaurants and lodging on the Web at www.granbury-tx.com.
  Granbury Opera House. Live performances in the opera house, built in 1886. On the square. 817/573-3779, www.granburyoperahouse.org.
  Lake Granbury, created in 1969 by damming the Brazos River. 817/573-1622
  Brazos Drive-In. 1800 W. Pearl St. 817/559-4473, www.thebrazos.com.
  Nutshell Eatery and Bakery. 122 E Pearl St. 817/279-8989.

Cleburne State Park features a spring-fed lake, water sports, camping. 5800 Park Road 21, Cleburne. 817/645-4215, www.tpwd.state.tx.us/park/cleburne.

Ride 7: The Northern Lakes
Riding the Oklahoma Border

If you like riding on gentle, rolling hills through woods and over lakes, you'll love this North Texas ride. Add in the network of reservoirs in the Red River and Trinity River systems, and you have a formula that spells bliss on a bike.

This ride takes you on back roads that wander through horse country, around lakes, over gently sloping hills, and through some of the most gorgeous scenery in the entire area. At times you'll be all alone, surrounded by trees and near the shores of some of the prettiest lakes in the entire system. All lakes in the Prairie and Lakes region are great for water sports and activities, but Lake Ray Roberts and Lake Texoma are among the most beautiful. These two call out to you to stop on their shores and breathe in the serenity.

After the mellow riding around these lakes, this route goes into the countryside, through some Main Street towns that have been restored to their original glory. There are plenty of populated areas to get whatever you might need, although this ride skirts around them as much as possible. So if you need something you are in luck, especially around Sherman and Denison.

For most of the ride, you will have a hard time remembering that you are just a stone's throw from the Dallas-Fort Worth metroplex. Like other rides in this book, there are places where the biggest hazard will be a slow-moving truck on a two-lane road. They will turn off soon, and then you will be free to race the wind again.

Getting Started: Pilot Point to Whitesboro

This ride starts in Pilot Point, a picturesque town near Lake Ray Roberts. One good way to get there is to take I-35 to Sanger, turn east on FM 455, and follow the lake around to Pilot Point.

Start the ride with a cup of coffee and homemade biscuits—or even a full breakfast—at Jay's Cafe and Museum on the square in Pilot Point. Jay and his wife Carolyn are very knowledgeable about the entire area. They have filled the little cafe with memorabilia of the town and everyday artifacts from the first half of the nineteen hundreds. There are no sterile display cases here; everything is displayed out in the open in a way that invites you to putter around and look. If you are there when Jay is not busy in the kitchen, he will sit down and entertain you with trivia and stories about all that he has collected. Almost apologetically Jay will tell you that Bonnie and Clyde never robbed a bank in Pilot Point. They did visit the town, and the bank at the corner was used in filming the Warren Beatty/Faye Dunaway movie about the infamous duo.

Take US 377 Business out of town. Turn north (left) on US 377 toward Tioga, hometown of "America's Favorite Singing Cowboy," Gene

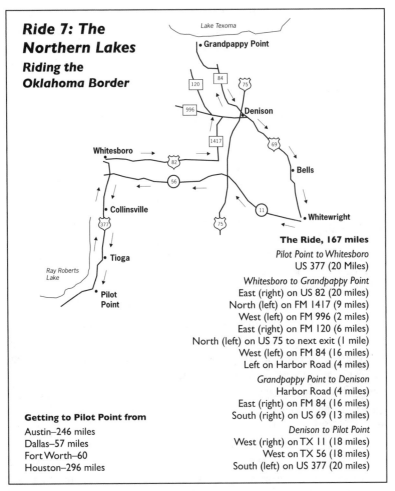

Ride 7: The Northern Lakes

Riding the Oklahoma Border

Lake Texoma

• Grandpappy Point

120 84 75

996 Denison

Whitesboro 82

56

69

• Bells

• Collinsville

377

11

75 • Whitewright

• Tioga

Ray Roberts Lake

Pilot Point

The Ride, 167 miles

Pilot Point to Whitesboro
US 377 (20 Miles)

Whitesboro to Grandpappy Point
East (right) on US 82 (20 miles)
North (left) on FM 1417 (9 miles)
West (left) on FM 996 (2 miles)
East (right) on FM 120 (6 miles)
North (left) on US 75 to next exit (1 mile)
West (left) on FM 84 (16 miles)
Left on Harbor Road (4 miles)

Grandpappy Point to Denison
Harbor Road (4 miles)
East (right) on FM 84 (16 miles)
South (right) on US 69 (13 miles)

Denison to Pilot Point
West (right) on TX 11 (18 miles)
West on TX 56 (18 miles)
South (left) on US 377 (20 miles)

Getting to Pilot Point from

Austin–246 miles
Dallas–57 miles
Fort Worth–60
Houston–296 miles

Autry. For the next six miles the straight road goes over small hills cascading through pastures and farmlands. It also passes Hidden Springs Winery, open for tastings on weekends. The highway crosses the first of several errant arms of Lake Ray Roberts shortly before Tioga. Since its population is only 754, the downtown business center is small, but you can bypass it all together by not taking the business spur of US 377. The farther north you go, the more trees.

Signs point the way to Lake Ray Roberts on your left. Created by a dam on the Elm Fork of the Trinity River, this lake is one of Texas's newest. Continue on US 377 for another fourteen miles to Whitesboro, where you'll pass a half-buried green station wagon, sort of like the autos at the famous Cadillac Ranch outside Amarillo. Ride the curves on US 377 Business, go under the railroad underpass, and pass it on your way into town.

Whitesboro to Grandpappy Point

The view is great from the top of the hill—even if it is a man-made hill—over the highway on the approach to US 82 East outside Whitesboro. The rolling four-lane divided highway for the twenty miles to Sherman makes for pleasant biking.

On the outskirts of Sherman, go north (left) on FM 1417 toward Pottsboro, Grayson County Airport, and Eisenhower State Park. Even though US 82 provides good riding, it is always refreshing to get off the main highway and out into the country again. The two-lanes-plus-shoulder road goes over hills and curves that surpass the main highway. In spite of a little light industry and an oil pumping station, there are still cattle grazing in the pastures, even close to town.

After about nine miles, turn west (left) on FM 996. Looking straight ahead as you come over some of the hills, you will see only sky and clouds. You almost feel like you are riding in paradise.

Pottsboro has deep ditches on either side of the road. A relatively sharp curve with a 35 mph speed limit marks the entrance into the town. The road zigzags through the community, so obey the 10 mph speed limit. Follow the FM 996 signs through town to the junction with FM 120.

FM 120 on the way to Denison is about eight miles of four-lane divided highway with very gentle curves and hills. After about a mile of city driving in Denison, turn north (left) onto US 75. At the first exit take a left onto FM 84 towards Lake Texoma. Boaters and fishermen may think this 89,000-acre lake was developed for them. Bikers know that curvy, isolated roads like these near the lake are where you can be one with your bike. You will think they were built specifically for your riding pleasure. Some curves are fairly sharp; occasionally a stop sign will jump out and surprise you.

To go to Eisenhower State Park, turn right at the sign and go the two miles to the park. On this short stretch, watch for the surprise stop sign that is easy to miss. Like many country blacktop roads, this one has no shoulder nor center stripe. You'll feel like you're in the middle of

Oklahoma is on the far shore of Lake Texoma at Grandpappy Point.

nowhere, for a very good reason—you are. The park, on rocky limestone bluffs above Lake Texoma, offers access to the lake and water sports, swimming, a six-mile hiking trail, picnicking, and camping.

To skip the park, keep going straight on FM 84 and continue another four miles toward Grandpappy Point. At Pappy's Grill and Grocery make a left onto Harbor Road. You can get tee shirts, hamburgers, fishing lures, ice, even a few groceries at Pappy's. Just past the store, the lake peeks above the trees on the right.

On weekends, especially in the summer, the lake will be dotted with the white sails of boats in the middle of the lake. When a sailor gets to his boat, he's where he wants to be. When a biker gets on his bike, he/she's where he/she wants to be. Although destinations are great, they are the icing on the cake. The thrill is in the getting there, not where you end up.

For the next four miles to Grandpappy Point, the narrow, two-lane blacktop road has trees and brush growing almost to the edge. There are lots of turns and little, bumpy hills, making the 15 mph speed limit reasonable.

A big sign and a fork in the road announce your arrival at Grandpappy Point. The right hand of the fork goes by the ships' store and row after row of docks. The left fork passes cabins and picnic areas on the way to the Point Restaurant at Lands End. If you keep going once you get to the restaurant you'll soon be known as a swimmer—next land, Oklahoma.

Grandpappy Point to Denison

At this point, you have to backtrack to get on FM 84 again. Fortunately, the riding from Grandpappy Point back has enough good features to make it fun a second time. Coming from the opposite direction makes the ride seem like a completely different road. When you get to US 75 you can leave the ride and take this major highway to your next destination. Or you can continue going straight on FM 84, past US 75, to ride and experience more of beautiful North Texas.

FM 84 narrows to two lanes with a wide shoulder after crossing US 75. The hills and long curves slope gently. After about a mile, continue straight through the stop sign. At the junction with US 69, about another mile down the road, turn south (right) onto a divided highway.

Denison, Texas, the birthplace of President Dwight D. Eisenhower, commemorates its native son at the Eisenhower Birthplace and Museum. The sister city of the hometown of the WWII general is Cognac, France. When you go through town, look at the murals painted on the walls on some of the buildings. There may be a bit of town traffic here, but it doesn't last for long. After crossing the overpass above the railroad track, go south (left) towards Bells on US 69.

Denison to Pilot Point

Once you see Denison in your rear-view mirror, you can enjoy the ups and downs and rounds and rounds of the hills and curves. Rails along the side of the road are there to protect traffic from the steep drops off the side. Even though you are enjoying the exhilaration of the ride, be careful and pay attention to the potential hazards. The agreeable riding continues down US 69 through Bells and on to Whitewright. Take a detour into the pretty, historic downtown, now being restored.

Turn west (right) onto TX 11, and continue riding over the very gentle hills and curves through these North Texas pasture lands. The easy rolling terrain through the countryside makes it hard to believe that you are riding a mere stone's throw from congestion of the Dallas-Fort Worth metroplex. When you return to Sherman, turn west (left) on TX 56. The views are great, and the light curves and little hills make this pleasurable riding. In some places you might see cattle grazing on one side of the road and horses on the other. The pastures behind the fences are dotted with scattered scrub trees.

At Whitesboro turn south (left) on US 377. Backtrack through Tioga and on to Pilot Point where you began. It's been fun!

Highlights Along the Way

Pilot Point. www.pilotpointonline.com.
Jay's Cafe and Museum has informal displays and photo gallery featuring the history of Pilot Point and the early 1900's. 110 W. Main St. 940/686-0158.
Farmer's and Merchant's Gallery. This building is the former bank used in the filming of the movie Bonnie and Clyde. Now it showcases Texas regional and contemporary art. 100 N Washington St.
Hidden Springs Winery. Tours on weekends. 256 N. Hwy 377. 940/686-2782, www.hiddenspringswinery.com.

Lake Ray Roberts. Camping facilities, 12-mile multi-use hiking trail and more are available at the Isle du Bois Unit. Four other areas also offer access to the lake. Off US 377 south of Pilot Point. 940/686-2148, www.tpwd.state.tx.us/park/rayrob.

Tioga.
Spirit of the West Resort. A full-service resort destination. 100 S. Texas St. 940/437-5000, www.spiritofthewestresort.net.

Whitesboro. http://whitesboro.texoma.net.

Hagerman Wildlife Refuge. Hwy 1417 at Lake Texoma. 903/786-2826, www.fws.gov/southwest/refuges/texas/hagerman/index.html.

Lake Texoma. www.laketexoma.com.
Eisenhower State Park. On the shores of Lake Texoma (www.laketexoma.com). Lake access, boat rentals, camping, and group facilities. 50 Park Rd. 20, Denison. 903/465-1956, www.tpwd.state.tx.us/park/eisenhow.
Grandpappy Point Marina. Gas dock, cabins, and the Point Restaurant. 132 Grandpappy Drive, Denison. 888/855-1972, www.grandpappy.com.
Point Restaurant. Overlooks Lake Texoma at Grandpappy Point Marina. 903/465-6376.

Denison. www.denisontx.com.
Dwight D. Eisenhower Birthplace and Museum. The home of the former president has been restored to its 1890s appearance. Picnicking on the grounds. 208 E. Day St. 903/465-8908, www.eisenhowerbirthplace.org.

Whitewright. Restored early 1900s buildings at the square.
Historical Museum, 202 S. Bond St.

Sherman. www.cityofsherman.org.

Ride 8: The Middle East to the Wild West
From Athens and Palestine to Gun Barrel City and Beyond

When Corsicana struck oil while drilling for water, a boom began. One of the state's first refineries was built here. Corsicana was the first city in Texas to have gaslights. Now the delicious, locally-made fruitcake brings the town its fame. Every year Deluxe Fruitcake is shipped from the Collin Street Bakery to every state in the union and to 300 foreign countries.

One of the interesting bits of Texas trivia is that so many towns have names reminiscent of grand cities from all over the world. This ride goes through a town named after a cradle of civilization, Athens. Of course, the Texas version differs from the Greek one; our Athens is also known as the "Black-eyed Pea Capital of the World." Another source of fame for Athens, Texas, is the New York (Texas) cheesecake made here. Be sure to sample a bit of several varieties when you are in town.

Palestine, another exotic-sounding stop, was not named after the Middle Eastern conflict-riddled area. Instead, this Texas sanctuary in the middle of thick woods and East Texas culture owes its name to the Illinois hometown of two early transplants to these parts.

Gun Barrel City sounds like the name of a town in an old-fashioned Western movie, or at least a town that should be somewhere near Langtry, Texas, where Judge Roy Bean ruled with his own brand of frontier justice. However, Gun Barrel City got its name from a mud road called Gun Barrel Lane, now TX 198, which provided a shortcut across Cedar Creek from Mabank to Trinidad. The town, which finally incorporated in the 1970s, chose "We shoot straight with you" as its motto and a rifle as its symbol.

Even though you probably won't see a shootout on Main Street at High Noon, you will see great roads that lead from one good stop to another. The choice will be hard; do you stop and enjoy all the area has to offer, or do you keep going straight on some great-riding roads through fabulous country?

Getting Started: Corsicana to Palestine

US 287 leaves Corsicana past the Russell Stover candy factory. Stop at the outlet store if you need a chocolate fix to get started. The two-lane road out of town is as smooth as luscious milk chocolate. Within a mile

Ride 8: The Middle East to the Wild West
From Athens and Palestine to Gun Barrel City and Beyond

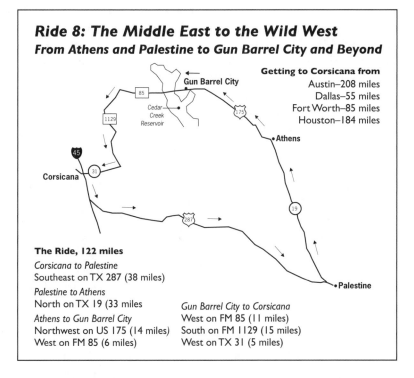

Getting to Corsicana from
Austin–208 miles
Dallas–55 miles
Fort Worth–85 miles
Houston–184 miles

The Ride, 122 miles

Corsicana to Palestine
Southeast on TX 287 (38 miles)

Palestine to Athens
North on TX 19 (33 miles)

Athens to Gun Barrel City
Northwest on US 175 (14 miles)
West on FM 85 (6 miles)

Gun Barrel City to Corsicana
West on FM 85 (11 miles)
South on FM 1129 (15 miles)
West on TX 31 (5 miles)

it begins rolling with gentle hills through grassy pasture land. After a wide curve, the road goes over a hill. Okay, so the hill is really an overpass above a railroad track, it rides like a hill, and the view from the top is as good as it gets around here. The road flattens out a bit around the small community of Mildred. Before long it's back to long, gentle hills through pastures and over streams.

The next signpost reads "Eureka." Except for the historical marker and public boat ramp, there's not much reason for a biker to stop in this little town. More likely, you'll say "Eureka, this ride is great!"

The scenery gets even better around the Richland Chambers Reservoir, a part of the Trinity River system. The bridge over this large water playground has two lanes plus shoulder. After crossing the lake the road curves, and the elevation begins to increase slightly. There are few crossroads as this stretch alternates between pasture and crop lands. Thick lines of trees in the distance mark the locations of streams and creeks running through the countryside.

Long, gentle hills, mostly straight with a few curves—some fairly sharp—make the next fifteen miles to Cayuga delightful riding. Watch out for road kill. The wildlife in the area sometimes wanders into the road. Although bikers don't get extra points for each dog or 'dillo they hit, other folks sometimes think they do.

Along the way are a few working oil fields producing homegrown fuel. Goats graze in the pastures. Outside Cayuga is a picnic area on the left with tables surrounded by tall pine trees, a cool place to stop. Just past it, a wildlife viewing area, part of the Engeling Wildlife Management Area, lets you observe furred and feathered creatures that might be passing by. Every few miles a house will break the breathtaking scenery of piney forests. The smooth road has gentle hills and long curves.

Be prepared for the red blinker at the intersection of US 287 and FM 321. After so many miles of bucolic riding, you may have been lulled into thinking you would never need to stop again. But Tennessee Colony is off the road a few miles, so there may be other vehicles at the intersection. Bikers may feel as if they are flying high around here until they see the sign to the National Scientific Balloon Facility at the intersection with FM 3224. Balloons as large as 300 feet in diameter are launched from here.

US 287 and TX 19 connect into a wide four-lane highway with shoulder on the way into Palestine. A large Welcome sign greets travelers coming into this town of 11,598 folks. A farmers' market at the Museum of East Texas Culture comes up just after the stoplight. Stop and absorb some Piney Woods culture or go straight on US 287, cross the railroad tracks, and venture into the old part of town. One-way streets lead to Courthouse Square, where professional offices now inhabit the older buildings across the streets. Follow the signs to Old Palestine, a collection of rustic buildings by a picturesque stream. Stop at Judy's Java Joint for a cup of "Inner Peace" as the sign in front of the historic building suggests.

Other places to eat include Ellenberger's Bakery, serving baked goods, tamale, and lunch all day, and The Ranch House, with its all-you-can-eat chicken fried steak buffet as well as a killer breakfast.

For something a little different, take the twenty-five mile ride through the dense East Texas woodlands to Rusk on the Texas State Railroad. Antique steam locomotives power vintage railroad cars along the route of Texas' skinniest park.

Palestine to Athens

Turn right on TX 19 N on the way out of town. The hills get a bit steeper and the trees thicker through this stretch of road towards Athens. The road, two lanes with a wide shoulder that makes taking the rolling hills and smooth curves easy, passes through some of the most appeal-

ing landscape in the state. This part of the Texas Forest Trails has little traffic, which is good, because there are too many curves to pass safely. Fortunately, the road occasionally widens to four lanes in case there is a pokey tractor holding up a line of cars and bikes.

The entrance to Camp Betty Perot Girl Scout Camp is to the left. Bois D'Arc, a community named after a

This scenic stream flows through Old Palestine.

type of tree that grows in the forests here, has a rich Native American heritage. The indigenous people prized the hard, flexible wood for making bows and for trading.

Occasional signs warn of trucks and emergency vehicles, so keep an eye open for them. The rapture of the ride can lead you to ignore everything else. The hills and curves are pleasurable, the vistas gorgeous, the road smooth. Enjoy this perfect stretch of road.

A few miles before entering Athens, you'll pass another beautiful picnic area tucked under some trees. Then the forests begin to thin a little. Horses graze in the pastures rather than cattle or goats, and miles of white board fencing line the road, rather than the barbed wire variety used to pen in the bovine herds.

TX 19 connects with US 175, a busy four-lane road, coming into Athens, population 11,297 and definitely part of the civilized world. Anything anyone might want from fast food to fuel is available here. Be sure to stop for a burger, since they were introduced at the 1904 St. Louis World's Fair by an Athens native, "Uncle" Fletcher Davis. The historical marker at the square honors him. Across the square is New York (Texas) Cheesecake, which was originally made in New York, Texas. It's worth a stop.

At the square, go west on US 175 to continue the ride.

Athens to Gun Barrel City

Where TX 31 and US 175 split, take the right fork as if going to Kaufman. A word of warning: the light is easy to miss at the split. Plant people, tree-huggers, gardeners, and nature lovers will want to visit the East Texas Arboretum and Botanical Society, about two miles ahead.

The long, rolling hills coming out of Athens go through more pasture land. US 175 narrows to two lanes, but occasionally it widens to four for passing. Spectacular views greet you at the apex of each hill.

Eustace, with a population of 798, a typical small town, offers visitors lots of fresh, homegrown fruit and vegetable at stands on the way into town. Purtis Creek State Park, on the right between Eustace and the exit to Gun Barrel City on FM 85, has a strictly-enforced catch and release fishing policy. So if you were planning on camping here and catching your supper, you better bring other vittles along. You can also enjoy hiking, picnicking, rest rooms, and heavily wooded, well-shaded campsites.

Gun Barrel City sits on the edge of Cedar Creek Reservoir, a large lake ripe for water sports. The community developed after creation of the reservoir forty years ago and incorporated a decade later to allow for the selling of beer and wine. It's a proud little town that has received several community achievement awards from the governor.

Since lots of people come here for the lake, Gun Barrel City has the atmosphere of a down-to-earth resort town. Keep in mind that the Sea Doos in the parking lots are a lot like motorcycles for the water.

Cattle grazing along the banks of the reservoir go to the edge to drink the water. Lily pads cover parts of the lake. The town has almost every franchise imaginable, but, just yards past the Wal-Mart parking lot, fishing piers stretch into the lake.

Gun Barrel City to Corsicana

The older, narrow bridge across the lake still fulfills its purpose of getting everyone to the other side. Boathouses and fishing piers fringe the edge of the lake, and an island glistens in the middle. A public boat ramp by the bridge is a good place to stop to put your feet in the water. Just make sure you can get your boots back on when you're finished.

After crossing the bridge, continue on FM 85 and enjoy the mild curves going through pasture land. A sign at the Trinity River Bridge says, "No Fishing from Bridge." No problem, the very narrow bridge has no room for you to stop for any reason.

At the junction with FM 1129, TX 85 goes to the right. Go straight, veering a little to the left to get on FM 1129. For the next fifteen miles until the junction with TX 31, take pleasure in the good, rural riding. With little traffic, few people, and good curves, you are just as likely to meet another motorcycle as you are to meet a car.

Enjoy the four-lane divided highway with broad shoulders of TX 31 W toward Corsicana. A few little hills and curves make this the perfect way to end a relaxing ride. At the intersection with I-45, turn left to go one mile south to the starting point or take off to other parts.

Highlights Along the Way

Collin Street Bakery. Home of "Deluxe" fruitcakes. The bakery sells cookies, pastries, rolls and more, including several varieties of the famous fruitcake. Ten-cent coffee and great restrooms. 401 W. 7th St., Corsicana. 800/248-3366, www.collinstreetbakery.com.

Richland Chambers Reservoir. www.tpwd.state.tx.us/fish/infish/lakes/richcham/lake_id.htm.

Engeling Wildlife Management Area. 11,000-acre wildlife habitat, day-use campsites. North of US 287 about 20 miles northwest of Palestine.

National Scientific Balloon Facility. Operated by NASA. Call 903/729-0271 to arrange a tour. www.nsbf.nasa.gov.

Palestine.

Museum of East Texas Culture. Historic displays in a 1915 schoolhouse, railroad memorabilia including a refurbished caboose. 400 Micheaux Ave. 903/723-1914, www.museumpalestine.org.

Judy's Java Joint. Coffee, lunch, and "Inner Peace." 213 E. Crawford St. 903/731-7097.

Ellenberger's Bakery. Baked goods, tamales, and lunch all day. 512 N. John St., Palestine. 903/729-0881, www.ohwy.com/tx/e/elbubaco.htm.

The Ranch House. Down-home lunch buffet, dinner, and breakfast. 305 E. Crawford St. 903/723/8778.

Texas State Railroad. Antique locomotives pull vintage cars 25 miles to Rusk through Texas' skinniest state park. Depot off US 84, three miles east of Palestine. 903/683-2561, www.tpwd.state.tx.us/park/railroad.

Athens.

New York (Texas) Cheesecake. Originally baked in New York, Texas, it is now located at the Square in Athens. 211 N. Palestine St. 903-677-6706, www.nytxccc.com.

Texas Freshwater Fisheries Center. Everything about freshwater fish. Nearly every variety of freshwater fish found in Texas can be seen in an aquarium exhibit of its natural habitat. Casting pond. 5550 Flat Creek Rd. (FM 2495) near Lake Athens, four miles east of Athens. 903/676-2277. www.tpwd.state.tx.us/fish/infish/hatchery/tffc.

East Texas Arboretum and Botanical Society. 100-acre arboretum with walking trails, beaver dams, and a picnic area. Off US 175 at 1601 Patterson Rd. 903/675-5630, www.eastexasarboretum.org.

Purtis Creek State Park. Catch and release fishing, swimming, camping, picnicking, and hiking. 14225 FM 316, three miles from US 175. 903/425-2332, www.tpwd.state.tx.us/park/purtis.

Cedar Creek Reservoir. Huge lake with numerous campsites, picnic areas, and swimming. www.tpwd.state.tx.us/fish/infish/lakes/cedarcrk/lake_id.htm.

Ride 9: The Lindbergh Legacy
New York to Paris

Charles A Lindbergh was the first to do it, and he will forever be in the history books for his achievement. You will feel like you have made history, too, if you follow his famous itinerary and zoom from New York to Paris. Of course, you will not need to leave the state of Texas to celebrate his famous journey.

The only thing Lindbergh saw on his flight was a lot of open ocean below and sky ahead. No wonder he did it nonstop. Going nonstop is absolutely not recommended on this ride. You will find something that excites you whether your second strongest passion, after your bike, is cheesecake in New York, fantasy birdhouses in Edom, trash and treasures in Canton, salt in Grand Saline, or any of the zillion other interesting sites you'll pass along the way.

Of course, there are a few differences between what he did and what you are about to do. Lindbergh went from west to east on his trip, but you will take off in the south and head north on yours. He departed from New York, New York, but this trip commences in New York, Texas. He flew over the Eiffel Tower and landed in Paris, France. This ride also ends in a city named Paris that boasts an Eiffel Tower, this one sports a giant version of the local headgear commonly worn by cowboys.

Lindbergh flew over salt water; you will ride over one of the world's largest salt domes. He flew like a bird; you will get to see some of the most unusual birdhouses ever made. You will have the opportunity to stop at lakes, quaint museums and shops, and to eat some good, hearty grub.

No trip to New York would be complete without some cheesecake. But to get some of the famous New York, Texas, variety, you have to stop at the square in Athens. Origi-nally the cheese-cake was made in New York, but the owners moved the bakery to the larger metropolis nearby. New York is located just outside of Ath-ens, at the inter-section of FM 804 and FM 607. Both roads cross US 175 going east out of Athens. Turn left at either intersection. If you are coming from Athens, FM 804 comes first and, at seven miles, is actually a few miles shorter than the FM 607 route. Both ways to New York are great for riding. Both are narrow

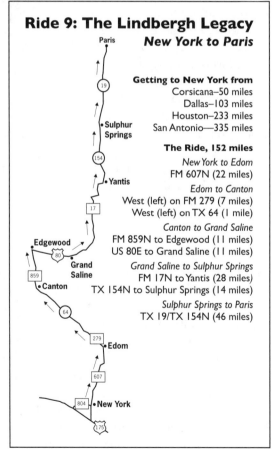

Ride 9: The Lindbergh Legacy

New York to Paris

Getting to New York from
Corsicana–50 miles
Dallas–103 miles
Houston–233 miles
San Antonio—335 miles

The Ride, 152 miles
New York to Edom
FM 607N (22 miles)

Edom to Canton
West (left) on FM 279 (7 miles)
West (left) on TX 64 (1 mile)

Canton to Grand Saline
FM 859N to Edgewood (11 miles)
US 80E to Grand Saline (11 miles)

Grand Saline to Sulphur Springs
FM 17N to Yantis (28 miles)
TX 154N to Sulphur Springs (14 miles)

Sulphur Springs to Paris
TX 19/TX 154N (46 miles)

country roads with curves, hills, and trees. The only ride better than the one getting to New York is the one you are about to take north to Paris.

Okay, you may be in New York, but this is Texas. That means mounting your saddle and riding on.

Getting Started: New York to Edom

New York has an official population in the double digits, the low double digits. With an official population of twelve, more cattle than people live in this pretty community.

Take FM 607 north out of town. For the next eighteen miles you will experience some of the best riding through some of the prettiest country in all of Texas. FM 607 is a typical farm-market road—narrow, no shoulder—with grass

There really is a New York, Texas.

growing up to the edge, little traffic, and only a few houses and other signs of human habitation along the side. The two-lane, no-passing zone road twists and curves and then turns back again.

Though not dangerous riding, you need to pay attention to the good turns that follow one after another. Some are sharp 90-degree angles, many have lowered speed limits, and the rest are just plain fun and gentle, the kind of riding that makes life worth living. Getting caught behind a slow-moving tractor presents one of the greatest hazards along this stretch.

Stay on FM 607, even when it zigzags. Follow the signs. Six miles before Edom you'll ride through Brownsboro, population 796. On the left you'll pass Echo Springs Blueberry Farms, one of several blueberry growers along the way. At Brownsboro turn left onto FM 314, following the sign to Edom. After six more miles of twisty roads and curves, the outskirts of Edom come into view. Straight, skyscraping pine trees grow in the yards of the houses along the side of the road just before the entrance to Edom. Blueberry Hill Farms has a picturesque red barn near the road that looks like the traditional red barn in children's books.

The heart of Edom beats where FM 314 dead-ends into FM 279. Visit some of the unique craftsmen who make and sell their wares at the intersection of this remote, rural artist's colony. You will not find welded horseshoe wine racks and other Texas kitsch. Instead, talented artists have their studios here.

Stop by to say "hey" to the potters Brown, Doug and Beth Brown; birdhouse maker extraordinaire Joe Hopps at Arbor Castle Birdhouses; or any of the other artisans. They are always glad to have folks drop by for a chat, all the better if you buy something, but certainly not a requirement. One biker babe fell in love with one of Joe's castle birdhouses. She managed to get it back to Dallas wrapped in bubble wrap and strapped to the passenger seat of her bike. The locals, as well as transient bikers, often stop next door at The Shed for hearty East Texas chow such as

Edom's Joe Hopps building one of his fantasy birdhouse castles.

chicken fried steak and salmon croquettes served up with homemade rolls and vegetables. Save room for pie.

Edom to Canton

Turn west (left) toward Ben Wheeler. Go straight on FM 279, or as straight as possible on the seven miles of twisty-turny road through pastures, blueberry fields, and nurseries. There is not much traffic and the road is smooth and flat. This is the area where master gardeners like to shop for plants. Unfortunately, trees don't ride well on the back of a bike.

Going through the community of Ben Wheeler is almost like still being in the country, except for the lower speed limit. Long sloping hills, trees, and great vistas make the riding out of town a sheer pleasure.

Turn left at the junction with TX 64 W toward Canton. Even though the traffic may be a bit heavier here, the long, sweeping hills and curves on this road make it one you will enjoy. The road passes Dawns View Ranch, its white fences going on forever. Cattle graze in pastures that have clusters of trees. Blueberries grow in adjacent fields.

The huge sign on the right welcoming visitors to First Monday tells you that this is Canton. First Monday actually happens on the Thursday through Sunday before the first Monday of every month. On that weekend thousands of venders sell everything from antiques to crafts, foods, junk, and anything else imaginable. There are more booths to shop than you'll have time for, and more things to buy than you'll have room for on your bike. Enjoy hiking the grounds in search of hidden treasures. On any day of the month, not just the First Monday weekend, you can stop in Old Town Canton for some good, old-time shopping.

Find the Canton Square Bed and Breakfast at the junction with FM 859. Take a right on FM 859, pass by the Blackwell House Museum, and head towards Edgewood.

Canton to Grand Saline

Coming out of Canton, enjoy the long, sloping descent with a curve at the bottom. However, a stop sign at the end of the curve brings you back to earth. Follow FM 859 N. A stop sign points the way back to Dallas, but the riding continues to be too good to leave the route unless you have a real emergency. The sloping hills, smooth curves, and a few rather tricky "S" switchbacks give this stretch enough excitement to make even an experienced biker feel blessed, but without making those with a little less experience too tremulous. In season, lots of stands sell fresh, home grown fruits and vegetables along the side of the road.

Big ranch houses act as a welcoming committee to bikers coming into Edgewood, a neat, well-kept community with big trees throughout the town. Edgewood Heritage Park features an historic village showing rural life as it was in the early part of the twentieth century. The claim-to-fame of Tom's Cafe, one of the structures moved to the park, is that Bonnie Parker and Clyde Barrow ate there.

At the light, turn right onto US 80 E toward Grand Saline, ten miles down the road. Four smooth lanes with broad shoulders make this an area to really let loose and run the speed limit as you sail over the long, sustained slopes. At the intersection of US 80 and TX 19, stop at the intersection with the four-way stop signs and blinking red light.

For the next eight miles to Grand Saline, the respectable curves continue. A few small businesses line the side of the road at Fruitvale. A train may even pass by on the tracks. This section of road has hills, trees, and not much traffic.

Grand Saline calls itself "The Salt of the Earth" because it sits atop a cylindrical underground salt dome that contains enough salt to last another 20,000 years. The Morton Salt Company does its best to make sure everyone has enough. The Salt Palace and Visitors Center, at the intersection of US 80 and TX 110, is located in a deceptively small building on the left. Packed inside is everything you ever wanted to know about salt and the Grand Saline salt dome. The helpful, informative staff can answer questions and give you additional, interesting information.

Take US 80 out of Grand Saline to the junction with FM 17 N and head for Alba.

Grand Saline to Sulphur Springs

Like a typical farm-to-market road, FM 17 is two lanes with no shoulder. It starts with a curve and a hill, indicating the beginning of some more good riding. The speed limit is 50 mph here, and for good reason. At the top of the hill, the road curves again. Then, about six miles outside of Grand Saline, two 90-degree curves come at you, back-to-back. The first goes to the right, the second to the left. Both curves suggest a top speed of 25 mph, very reasonable under the circumstances. The curves continue coming, one after another. Riding does not get much better than this.

The road widens a bit on the bridge over the Sabine River. One nice thing about bridges going across a river or reservoir: there is never any cross traffic. This road generally has very little of that anyway, but there may be times when there is some. On the other side of the river, the curves and hills continue all the way to Alba. Houses with neat yards mark the entrance to town. Follow FM 17 through the intersection with US 69, but turn left at the stop sign. Follow the arrows to stay on FM 17 through another stop sign, then take off for Yantis, thirteen miles ahead.

The Lake Fork Reservoir is a couple of miles ahead. It's another one of the beautiful man-made lakes in Texas, custom designed for pleasure as well as for environmental purposes. Fishing piers and boathouses are built out over the water. Once again, any cross traffic will go under the bridge and not affect your progress. The fourth crossing of the reservoir is a mile-and-a-half-long causeway. The area caters to fishermen who are free spirits, much like bikers, so stop anywhere that looks appealing. FM 17 starts to get a little rougher, but the terrain is still hilly, curvy, and pretty.

In Yantis, turn left to go to Sulphur Springs on TX 154 W at the stop sign and blinking red light. The road to Sulphur Springs is fourteen miles of long sweeping hills and gentle curves through pastures and trees. Meeting a car every five minutes or so will seem like a lot of traffic compared to the amount of traffic up to this point. Occasionally the two-lane road widens to four to allow for passing, important for overtaking slow-moving farm vehicles.

Sulphur Springs to Paris

Even without the sign announcing the Sulphur Springs Livestock and Dairy Auction every Thursday, all the cattle and stockyards along the road coming into town tell you about one of the major industries here. Stop for lunch or a cold ice cream treat at The Creamery in the Southwest Dairy Center Museum. While there, try one of the hands-on exhibits. Then follow TX 154 W around the courthouse square, where you will see the war memorial, dedicated to fallen residents of the area.

The Eiffel Tower, Texas-style, in Paris.

History buffs should also stop at the Hopkins County Museum and Heritage Park. Original historic houses, shops, and mills dating as far back as the 1870s have been moved here. More will be coming.

At the point where TX 154 joins in with TX 19, Sulphur Springs will be in your rear view mirror. Head north.

Paris is only thirty-five miles ahead. The road flattens out some, but there are still some small hills and curves through pasture land and trees. Make tracks and move here, while still obeying all the speed limits and other laws. Hike, play in the water, or stay overnight in a cabin or campsite at Cooper Lake State Park, off the road a bit. You'll see the signs pointing the way.

Enjoy riding along this stretch. The smooth, mostly flat roadbed rides above the surrounding landscape. Pastures gradually become cropland as the terrain becomes more prairie than wooded.

Turn right when TX 19 N / TX 24 comes to a dead end. After fifteen more miles of good riding, you'll land in Paris. When you get there, turn right at the mid-nineteenth century Evergreen Cemetery onto Jefferson Street to go to the Love Civic Center. At the civic center, "The Second Largest Eiffel Tower in the Second Largest Paris" stands tall and wears a red cowboy hat. Obviously proud of its namesake, the City of Paris built its version of the Eiffel Tower in 1993, and added the hat five years latter. The Texas Paris and Eiffel Tower have been a destination for travelers ever since. For more European sights, retrace the way to Evergreen Cemetery and turn right. The Italian marble Culbertson Fountain flows in the middle of the town square.

Instead of returning to the beginning by a different route, as do most of the rides in this book, the Lindbergh Ride ends here. Choose your own way back home, since it was probably some place other than New York.

Highlights Along the Way

Edom. A number of artists have their studios at the intersection of FM 279 and FM 314. The mix may change, but these have been around for a while. www.seekonsearch.com/TX/Edom.

Potters Brown. Handmade pottery, especially dinnerware in rich colors by Doug and Beth Brown. 903/852-6473.

Arbor Castle Birdhouses. Whimsical, castle-inspired birdhouses by artist Joe Hopps. 903/852-7893, www.arborcastlebirdhouses.com.

The Shed Cafe. Home style Texas food. 903/852-7791.

Canton.

First Monday Trade Days. 7,000 vendors gather on 300 acres to sell almost everything imaginable. Trade Days are on the weekend before the first Monday of each month. Downtown Canton on TX 19. 903/567-2991, www.firstmondaycanton.com.

Blackwell House Museum. Oldest House in Canton, built in the 1880s. 903/567-2991, www.cantontx.com.

Edgewood Heritage Park. Village recreating life in the early twentieth century with original buildings moved to the park. North Houston and Elm streets in Edgewood, 4 blocks north of US 80 on FM 859. 903/896-1940, www.vzinet.com/heritage.

Salt Palace and Museum. Everything about salt and the Grand Saline salt dome. US 80 and TX 110 in Grand Saline. 903/962-5631, www.saltpalace.org.

Lake Fork Reservoir. Part of the Sabine River Authority. 903/878-2262, www.sra.dst.tx.us/aboutsra/lfd.asp.

Sulphur Springs. www.sulphurspringstx.org.
   Courthouse Square. 118 Church St. Hopkins County Courthouse. Romanesque Revival, built in 1894; War Memorial, dedicated to locals fallen in service to their country.
   Southwest Dairy Center Museum. Everything about the dairy industry, including The Creamery, which serves lunch and ice cream treats. 1210 Houston St. 903-439-6455, www.swdairycenter.org.

   Hopkins County Museum and Heritage Park. 416 N. Jackson St. Eleven acres of original historic houses, shops, and mills have been moved to the site. 903/885-2387, www.hopkinscountytx.org/history/heritage-museum.htm.

Cooper Lake State Park. Cabins, camping, hiking trails, sand volleyball and water sports. 903/395-3100, www.tpwd.state.tx.us/park/cooper.

Paris. www.paristexas.com.
   Eiffel Tower. Replica of the famous landmark, Texas-style. Love Civic Center, Jefferson Rd at S. Collegiate Dr.
   Evergreen Cemetery. Nineteenth century cemetery. S. Church St. at Jefferson Rd.
   Culbertson Fountain. Downtown plaza, Main Street at Lamar Avenue.

Piney Woods

When the world gets to be too much, some people head for the beach, others for the mountains, others go to the forests. The last category of folks, as well as anyone else who enjoys the vast greenness of opulent East Texas, go to the Piney Woods. Huge stands of tall, straight pine trees populate this region, hence giving it its name.

This region stretches along the East Texas-Louisiana border from the Gulf Coast region north to the Red River. At one time the Big Thicket, just north of Beaumont, covered three and a half million acres of forest and supported a whole cornucopia of diverse plants and wildlife. Then the logging industry came.

Fortunately, efforts are now being made to preserve the natural abundance of the area. The Sam Houston, Davy Crockett, and Sabine national forests are all located in this region, as is the Big Thicket National Preserve. Lakes and reservoirs also dot the area, making it one of the most luxuriant regions in the state. Compared to the arid deserts of the western and even central areas of the state, this is one of the greenest parts of Texas.

Because of the abundant natural resources, early Native Americans and Spaniards inhabited these parts. Some of the earliest Texas settlements are here, and many important events in Texas history occurred in these forests. Towns have such intriguing names as Quicksand and Uncertain. Jefferson comes populated with ghosts from times past. Somehow, it all seems fitting when riding the Piney Woods.

Today the area sports great roads through peaceful surroundings. The idyllic nature of the area has generally been preserved. Most definitely, the riding rates among the best.

Ride 10: The Raven Ride
Sam Houston National Forest

When traffic, superhighways, and crowds get to be too much, the best thing to do is escape the congestion of life by riding through an unspoiled, protected forest. Not far from Houston exists one of the best places for this type of ride, Sam Houston National Forest. With more than 160,000 acres of forest land intermingled with privately owned timberland and more than 120 miles of hiking trails for leg-stretching, a biker can't help but feel relaxed after taking this easy ride. Kick back and enjoy.

Even though humans have occupied this area for more than twelve thousand years, the forest bears the name of a legendary Texas hero who hails from nearby Huntsville. Although every Texas schoolchild knows that Sam Houston was commander in chief of the Army of the Republic of Texas, victor at the Battle of San Jacinto, a president of the Republic of Texas, and, later, a US Senator from Texas, he was a controversial figure during his lifetime. Some contemporaries disagreed with his fair treatment of the Indians and his stand against secession during the Civil War.

Regardless of his politics or other stories that circulated about him, Sam Houston is most certainly a larger-than-life hero, as the world's tallest statue, just north of this ride on I-45, implies.

If you look off the road into the dense piney woods of the Sam Houston National Forest, you can almost imagine the Texas general, named Raven by his adopted Cherokee father, Chief Oolooteko, and his band of renegades fighting here for Texas' independence. You can sense what it would be like to gallop through these thick forests on horseback. On this ride you will experience the beauty and thrill of the general's territory.

Getting Started: New Waverly to Coldspring

Unless you're into gymnastics and want to stop by his Olympic training ground to say "hey" to Bela Karoly, ride on through New Waverly. As soon as you cross the railroad tracks you'll catch your first glimpse of the Piney Woods. Then the gentle curves and hills begin. The "Limited Sight Distance" sign warns that you need to adjust your riding accordingly. The corkscrew curves start coming, and, for a while at least, there is no such thing as a straightaway. This isn't a particularly dangerous stretch, but you have to watch what you are doing. You might see other bikers on this bit of road; it is a favorite of the locals.

Don't count on riding on the shoulder; there is no such thing around here. You'll pass through some of the more interesting-sounding Texas towns like Pumpkin and Evergreen. As you get closer to Coldspring,

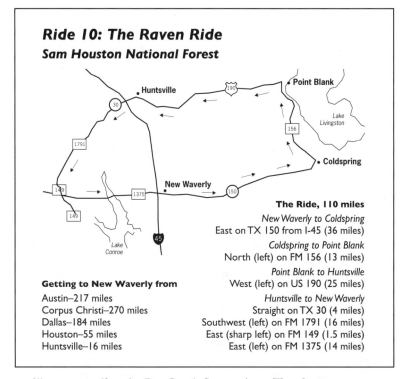

Ride 10: The Raven Ride
Sam Houston National Forest

Huntsville

Point Blank

Lake Livingston

Coldspring

New Waverly

The Ride, 110 miles
New Waverly to Coldspring
East on TX 150 from I-45 (36 miles)
Coldspring to Point Blank
North (left) on FM 156 (13 miles)
Point Blank to Huntsville
West (left) on US 190 (25 miles)
Huntsville to New Waverly
Straight on TX 30 (4 miles)
Southwest (left) on FM 1791 (16 miles)
East (sharp left) on FM 149 (1.5 miles)
East (left) on FM 1375 (14 miles)

Lake Conroe

Getting to New Waverly from
Austin–217 miles
Corpus Christi–270 miles
Dallas–184 miles
Houston–55 miles
Huntsville–16 miles

you'll see a cutoff to the Big Creek Scenic Area. This features many varieties of vegetation you can see in one place, especially if you take one of the four hiking loops. Take the detour if you want to see some more beautiful country or if you are ready to take a hike to stretch your legs.

Coldspring to Point Blank

At Coldspring, go north (left) on FM 156 towards Point Blank. You'll go through what Yankees imagine when they think of rural, agricultural Texas. You'll see a few houses with picturesque signs over the driveways announcing the name of the farm or ranch. A good road and not much traffic make this idyllic riding. You'll probably see more cattle than people. You'll also see evidence of the logging industry. In places the stand of trees gets thinner, but the selective pruning lets those remaining pines grow taller and straighter.

You'll also see Lake Livingston, one of Texas's many man-made lakes. There are a number of great views of the lake and marinas. To visit Lake Livingston State Park you will want to go to the eastern side of the lake, closer to the town on Livingston itself. Like most state parks, this one offers camping, restrooms, showers, and water sports.

US 190 from Point Blank will take you to the other side of the lake for a peaceful, watery detour. While there, you might want to visit the Alabama-Coushatta Indian Reservation. Sam Houston was instrumental in creating the reservation in the 1850s for these two Southern forest tribes. This part of the Piney Woods is known as the Big Thicket, and it certainly is just that.

One rumor claims that Point Blank got its name when John Wesley Harden shot his adversary at point blank range during a gunfight here. Like all rumors, this one may have some foundation in truth, or it may be total fabrication.

Point Blank to Burton

You'll see a sign that points the way to Huntsville. Make the turn to stay on FM 156, but, before you can blink, you'll have to make a sharp left on US 190. Follow the signs. If you are thirsty at this point, you might meet other bikers at the Hilltop Icehouse. Check out the parking lot to see how many of your compadres are here. US 190 provides good riding with gentle hills and curves. It starts with four lanes but narrows to two with a wide shoulder before long. You are still riding in the Sam Houston National Forest, so the scenery remains woody and green.

Huntsville may be home to Sam Houston University and several state prisons, but it still feels like a small town. Signs point the way to the two major landmarks of the area. The Sam Houston Memorial Museum complex is right across the street from the university campus on fifteen acres originally belonging to the general. The complex includes two period-furnished homes, his law office, a museum, and a romantic park.

This ride passes by the square and the Walker County Courthouse. The courthouse, built in 1888, was destroyed by a fire eighty years later. One reason the building could not be saved was that the only fire alarm was located on top of the courthouse. By the time the volunteer fire department arrived, it was too late.

Cafe Texan on the square is a good place for a hearty Texas meal. It serves some of the best chicken-fried steak around and is the oldest continually operating cafe in Texas. A number of marked historic buildings are located around the courthouse square. In Huntsville you can find a wide variety of fuel, food, services, and lodging.

Huntsville to New Waverly

US 190 becomes TX 30 when you cross over I-45. You'll immediately feel the difference. Even though you're still technically in town, you know you won't be for long. Of course, if you are already mellow and need to return to the rest of the world, take I-45 north or south to your destination.

If you want an interesting side trip, go north (right) on I-45 to Exit 118 and the Texas Prison Museum, one of the more unusual museums

you will ever visit. "Old Sparky," the famous Texas Electric Chair, is on display, as well as other mementos from the 150 years of the state prison system. This museum is definitely not a feel-good, lily-white museum. Instead, you'll see a replica of a prison cell, illegal weapons made by inmates, and other exhibits that might be a bit disturbing, even if extremely intriguing.

From TX 30, turn left on FM 1791 to ride gentle curves and hills again. The easy-riding road sports just enough houses and civilization to keep you grounded, yet not enough to crowd you. A few really good hills

Peaceful picnic areas await in Sam Houston National Forest.

and curves that are fun make the road pleasurable without being dangerous. Take a left at the stop sign at FM 149. A small hill blocks the view, so be careful when making that turn.

Take another left onto FM 1375 and follow the sign to New Waverly. Once again you'll be on another fine riding road with plenty of mild hills and gentle curves. Just don't get off the road, as the slope off the side is pretty steep. Do not pass that occasional slow driver when visibility is low.

You'll cross Lake Conroe, another one of the region's picturesque man-made lakes. Stop at one of the designated parking areas to stretch your legs on a scenic hiking trail. There are four connecting loops that make up a 40-mile trail here. That's certainly enough to get any kinks out of anyone's cramped legs. There are also showers, restrooms, and fishing.

If you ride during the right time of the year, you might see one of the endangered bald eagles that winter here. If you stop to hike during hunting season, make sure you're wearing highly visible clothing. Black biker duds or traditional camo gear might just get you mistaken for whatever is in season.

When you hit I-45 you can go on to Houston or Dallas or anywhere else, north or south. New Waverly, where this ride began, is only a mile farther south.

Highlights Along the Way

Sam Houston National Forest. More than 160,000 acres of protected forest and wildlife management intermingled with privately owned timberland. The boundaries between the two are marked with signs and red paint. Only the national lands, not the privately owned areas, are open to the public. Camping, picnicking, and water sports available. Livingston. 936/327-8487, 877/444-6777 for the National Reservation Service; http://www.southernregion.fs.fed.us/R8/recreation/sam_houston/samhouston_gen_info.shtml.

Lake Conroe. www.tourtexas.com/lakeconroe.

Big Creek Scenic Area. Four loops of hiking trails, camping, picnicking, swimming, and showers are here in addition to the natural beauty.

Lake Livingston State Park is on the eastern shores of Lake Livingston in pine and hardwood forests. Camping, restrooms, showers, hiking, nature trails, and water sports. Park Road 65. www.tpwd.state.tx.us/park/lakelivi.

Alabama-Coushatta Indian Reservation is home of these two Southern forest tribes which is located in the dense wooded area of the Big Thicket. Scenic camping areas, Indian culture, train tour. 936/563-1100. www.alabama-coushatta.com.

Point Blank. Hilltop Icehouse, Highway 190. 936/377-2506.

Huntsville.
Sam Houston University. www.shu/edu.
Sam Houston Memorial Museum complex dedicated to the life and times of the Texas hero. Two homes, law office, museum, romantic park, and more. 1836 Sam Houston Ave. 936-294-1832, www.shu.edu/~smm_www/GenInfo.
Cafe Texan. 1120 Sam Houston Ave. 936/295-2381.
Texas Prison Museum. Exhibits from the state's 150 years of prison history, including the Texas Prison Rodeo, famous inmates, the Carrasco prison siege, and more. 491 TX 75 N., I-45 exit 118. 936/295-2155, www.txprisonmuseum.org.

Sam Houston statue and Visitors Center. The world's tallest statue of an American hero can be seen from I-45 from a distance of 6.5 miles. 7600 Texas 75S, I-45 exit 109 or 112. 800/289-0389, www.samhoustonstatue.org.

Whistler Bed & Breakfast. 906 Ave. M. 800/404-2834, www.thewhistlerbnb.com.

Bluebonnet Bed & Breakfast. 1374 White Rd. 936/295-2072.

Kaldi's Coffee House. 1627 Sam Houston Ave. 936/436-0451.

Ride 11: The Far East
Sabine National Forest, Toledo Bend Reservoir, Even a Little Louisiana

One of the best parts of The Far East is getting to the beginning at Newton. No matter where you come from, you will ride through miles of beautiful East Texas piney woods. This ride gets you off the sterile interstates and monotonous US highways. It will take you on state highways and farm-to-market roads that cut through thick stands of Virginia shortleaf pines and yellow pines. At times you will feel as if you are traveling through deep canyons of trees with solid walls of vegetation towering above. The immenseness of the forest makes even the most powerful bike seem insignificant.

The apex of this ride, the turning-around point, is the Toledo Bend Reservoir, which forms the Texas-Louisiana boundary. It lies about as far east you can get and still stay in Texas. This ride crosses the lake and travels a little more than thirty miles along the reservoir in Louisiana.

Although this book is about Lone Star rides, even the proudest Texans who love bikes will admit that Texas does not have a monopoly on good riding. No border patrol will question you as you cross the boundary, and passports are not needed to return home. So ride over to the next state, and compare the roads. You will notice a difference, and you will also enjoy a different perspective on East Texas.

Enjoy the roads and the scenery on this ride, because this is not a destination ride with lots of sightseeing. The Far East Ride covers a relatively short distance, so, even if you have to travel miles to get to the beginning, you can still do the loop and get back in an afternoon or a day. Although there are lots of curves and turns, these roads are not as technically difficult as some of the others in this book. With proper caution, even those with less than stellar experience can manage quite well.

So stop, breathe in the fresh air, and ride on.

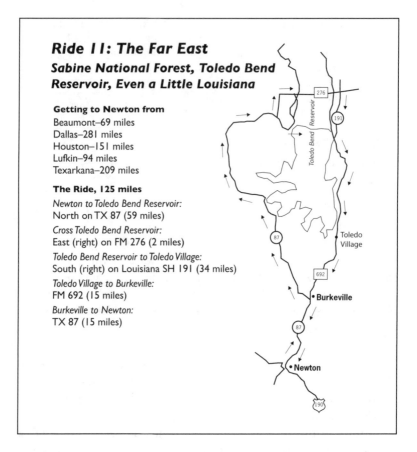

Ride 11: The Far East
Sabine National Forest, Toledo Bend Reservoir, Even a Little Louisiana

Getting to Newton from
Beaumont–69 miles
Dallas–281 miles
Houston–151 miles
Lufkin–94 miles
Texarkana–209 miles

The Ride, 125 miles
Newton to Toledo Bend Reservoir:
North on TX 87 (59 miles)
Cross Toledo Bend Reservoir:
East (right) on FM 276 (2 miles)
Toledo Bend Reservoir to Toledo Village:
South (right) on Louisiana SH 191 (34 miles)
Toledo Village to Burkeville:
FM 692 (15 miles)
Burkeville to Newton:
TX 87 (15 miles)

Getting Started: Newton to Toledo Bend Reservoir

No matter which of the roads you ride into Newton, before long you will come to an intersection with TX 87. This is definitely biker-friendly territory. Somewhere along this route you will pass other motorcycles. If you meet them around Newton they may be going to Sawmill Town USA, home of the Road Kill Cafe, Iron Horse Saloon, and a spring Chopper Rally. When there is live music or a DJ, you can join a host of other bikers and ordinary folks for some partying.

To get on with this ride, however, head north on TX 87 toward Newton. With a population of almost two thousand, you won't get lost and can easily find your way out of town. Very quickly after getting on TX 87 going north you will cross Caney Creek, go around the curve, and then ride deep into the woods. You will see a lot of curves, woods, hills, and bridges on this ride. Fortunately, those are the ingredients for a perfect afternoon on a motorcycle.

Feel the freedom, but don't stop for hitchhikers. This is a prison area. Even though it is a minimum-security prison, don't risk it.

After a few long curves and hills, you'll cross Quicksand Creek, which, as you might guess, has quicksand. At one time the town of Quicksand, named after the creek, was thought to be the geographical center of the county. The county seat was located here until a survey proved that it was not the center, and the courthourse was moved. Except for the sign, you might never know you had passed through Quicksand.

This typical two-lane-deep East Texas state highway has no shoulder. It feels like a country farm-to-market road even though it's not one. The hills and curves are calm enough to take with a little speed. There are few houses and even fewer signs of congestion. You'll have to wait until you get to Burkeville, about fourteen miles north of Newton, for fuel or drinks.

Burkeville was once a place where stagecoaches stopped so travelers could eat at the Harrel House, built in 1865. Now the restaurant is called the Round Table Inn, named for its large, hand-made lazy Susan table that seats 12 to 15 people. With a population of a little over 500 residents, the town has limited gas and food, but it has a curve worthy of a lower speed on the way out of town on TX 87. The curves become sharper and the hills become hillier as you leave Burkeville and ride deeper into the woods. There are speed limit signs for the more challenging curves.

Don't try to pass on the windy, twisty curves. If you get stuck behind a slow vehicle, a hazard in rural areas where time passes at a different rate than it does for the rest of us, and you feel an urgent need to pass, wait for one of the periodic stretches where the road widens to four lanes. Occasional logging trucks present another hazard on the road around here. Watch out for them, because they certainly won't be looking out for you. Since logging is very important around here, give them some leeway. Signs point out the plant entrances and other places the trucks are likely to be, so you can be prepared.

The fences along the side of the road have signs every so often warning that the area is posted. Do not climb over the fence under any circumstances. Hunting is on the other side. You don't want to be mistaken for a doe, a deer, or a dove, depending on the season.

Before and after you go through Mayflower, enjoy the corkscrews, switchbacks, and all sorts of twisty turns. "Damn good!" and "Awesome ride!" are what a couple of bikers said about this stretch. This is the way riding should be.

At Six Mile Creek you'll get a glimpse of what the Toledo Bend Reservoir is all about. The gigantic lake was created by building a dam on the Sabine River, a major joint effort by Texas and Louisiana. The reservoir forms the boundary between the two states. A vast number of recreational areas surround the reservoir. Like all areas around a major lake, this caters to the crowd that loves boating, fishing, and all sorts of water activities. These folks have a lot in common with bikers, so you can get beverages, bait, and fuel.

Then the road goes back into the woods and the landscape gets back to first-rate riding with hills and curves. Instead of a shoulder there is a drop-off off the side of the road.

The trees get thicker off the side of the road as you enter the Sabine National Forest. In the forest you will have some straightaways, but there are enough curves to keep the ride interesting as you approach Hemphill. When you get to Hemphill, take the sharp right turn to stay on TX 87. This town of 1,100 people is built in the middle of the forest. Tall trees and houses scattered throughout the business areas along the highway make even going through town a pleasure.

The Indian Mounds Recreation Area outside of town is an interesting detour. It has a number of good campsites, open all year. Don't confuse the Indian Mounds Recreational Area with the Indian Mounds Wilderness Area; there are signs to both. The Wilderness Area is just that, a wilderness, complete with huge populations of insects, not a recreation area. Be sure to take the detour you intend to take. Actually, the Indian mounds are not really the handiwork of prehistoric people. Recently researchers have concluded that the mounds are the result of natural geologic processes.

You'll pass through some ranchland with cattle and ponds, then once again you'll be back in the trees with more curves. Just up ahead, the Toledo Bend Reservoir forms the Texas and Louisiana border. This recreational paradise has all sorts of facilities for sportsmen as well as bikers.

Toledo Bend Reservoir forms the boundary between Texas and Louisiana.

One of the best places to stop is the Lakeview Campground, located at the trailhead for the Trail Between the Lakes. The last half-mile of the road to the campground is not paved, so be careful. The Trail Between the Lakes is a 28-mile long hiking trail that winds through the Sabine National Forest. Rectangular aluminum tags attached to trees mark the trail. Even if you are not a serious hiker, commune with nature here, and enjoy the outdoors.

For more downright good riding, continue across the bridge into Louisiana. Turn east (right) on TX 21 at Milam to take the bridge to the other side of the reservoir.

Toledo Bend Reservoir to Toledo

The next thirty-four miles may be in Louisiana, but the riding is still terrific. Make a right (south) turn onto Louisiana State Highway 191 to find your way back to Texas. Even though Texans like to think everything is bigger and better than anywhere else in the world, even the proudest Texas bikers have to admit that this is the kind of terrain that puts pleasure in motorcycle riding. The mild curves and hills keep coming, one after another, with an occasional corkscrew and switchback. The curves are banked so you can take them with a bit of speed and safety, but there are just enough of them to make passing dangerous. Even when the curves eventually straighten out, the hills still follow one after another.

On your right you'll have great views of the Toledo Bend Reservoir. In the distance to your left you can see down into valleys and up into the hills on the other side. Cyclists also like the hills of Louisiana, so watch out for them in the bicycle lane. They are working too hard to take the hills to enjoy it the way you are. About two miles before the Texas border is the Toledo Bend Resort. It has cabins, camping, a shower house, picnicking, and a sandy beach.

When you cross into Texas, Louisiana 191 turns into FM 692. The hydroelectric dam on the Texas side of the Sabine River and Toledo village marks the end of the jaunt out of state.

Toledo Village to Burkeville

If you are traveling this stretch at any time other than high noon, it will be shady, and the tall trees on both sides of the road keep it cool as well. This run has appealing scenery and calm riding, with just enough curves and hills to keep it interesting, perfect for cruising.

The road gets curvier as you get closer to Burkeville. Turn west (right) onto TX 63, which will get you to TX 87. Take TX 87 south to Newton.

Highlights Along the Way

Sawmill Town US. Includes Road Kill Cafe and Iron Horse Saloon; bar serves only set-ups so BYOB. Entertainment. On US 190, 2.3 miles west of junction with TX 87 at Newton. 409/379-3851.

Sabine National Forest. Borders the Toledo Bend Reservoir. Numerous recreational areas, including Indian Mounds Wilderness Area, Lakeview Campground, Trails between the Lakes. www.toledo-bend.com.

Indian Mounds Recreation Area. Developed and undeveloped campsites open year round. Along the way you will see signs to Indian Mounds Wilderness Area, which is a wilderness, not a recreation area. Visitors can hike to the Indian mounds. From junction of TX 87 and TX 83 in Hemphill, take TX 83 E 7 miles to FM 3382, turn South on FM 3382 and go 3.9 miles to Indian Mounds Recreation Area.

Lakeview Campground. Camping, water, chemical flush toilets located at the trailhead for Trail between the Lakes. Four miles east on FM 2928; the last half mile is unpaved.

Trail between the Lakes. 28-mile hiking trail marked by rectangular aluminum tags on trees. It begins near Lakeview Campground.

Toledo Bend Reservoir. Created by a dam on the Sabine River to form the boundary between Texas and Louisiana. Numerous recreational sites in the area. www.toledo-bend.com.

Toledo Bend Resort: Cabins, camping, shower house, picnicking, and sandy beach on the Louisiana shores of Toledo Reservoir. 350 Toledo Resort Dr., Anacoco, LA. 337/286-9257, www.toledobendresort.com.

Ride 12: A Ghostly Ride
Jefferson and the Lakes

During its heyday in the nineteenth century, Jefferson was a bustling river port that rivaled Galveston in the amount of cargo arriving and leaving the docks. Wealthy entrepreneurs and businessmen built lavish homes, many of which are still standing today. In the late 1800s the great decline began, and Jefferson's population went from a high of around thirty thousand to its current level of just more than two thousand. This number, however, counts only those souls actually living with a human form.

Jefferson has been called a haunted city. Strange events and ephemeral sightings have convinced many that unexplained spirits actually do reside here. The stories are numerous, though some town folks deny that anything supernatural occurs in Jefferson. Others have accepted the spirits and reside pleasantly with their ghostly friends. As for what you want to believe, try visiting one of the "haunted" sites and decide for yourself.

Most of the haunted entities are not here to harm the living. Most of the time, they do not need human intervention in their particular quest and will ignore those still alive. Many times they are quite benevolent and protect humans from danger. So if you see spirits, even if you do not believe they exist, relax and enjoy their presence.

When you leave Jefferson on this ride you will go through dense forests and then to Caddo Lake, ripe with cypress trees dripping with long strands of Spanish moss. The setting is perfect for haunted souls to make their presence known. Even if you do not actually see one, you can almost feel them lurking in the shadows.

Then this ride takes you back through Jefferson on your way to Lake O' the Pines, a more traditional lake. All around the area are bayous and swamps and soft hills and curves. Not only is this part of Texas beautiful and mysterious, it also provides good riding.

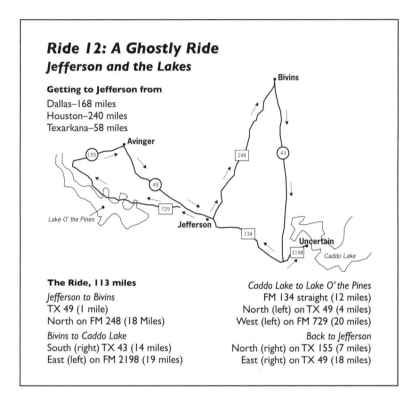

Ride 12: A Ghostly Ride
Jefferson and the Lakes

Getting to Jefferson from

Dallas–168 miles
Houston–240 miles
Texarkana–58 miles

The Ride, 113 miles

Jefferson to Bivins
TX 49 (1 mile)
North on FM 248 (18 Miles)

Bivins to Caddo Lake
South (right) TX 43 (14 miles)
East (left) on FM 2198 (19 miles)

Caddo Lake to Lake O' the Pines
FM 134 straight (12 miles)
North (left) on TX 49 (4 miles)
West (left) on FM 729 (20 miles)

Back to Jefferson
North (right) on TX 155 (7 miles)
East (right) on TX 49 (18 miles)

Getting Started: Jefferson to Bivins

As you are cruising the streets of Jefferson, you will most likely notice some motorcycles parked on Austin Street. The riders of those bikes are probably in Auntie Skinner's Riverboat Club & Restaurant.

Your kind congregates here, so you know the beer must be cold and the food good. There are no known ghosts who haunt Auntie Skinner's.

If you want ghosts, some of the best places to meet up with one are the Hotel Jefferson, Falling Leaves Bed and Breakfast, Lamacheo's Italian Restaurant, and the Big Cypress Coffee House. Or you can drop by to tour The Grove, a private residence, that has been called "The Most Haunted House in Jefferson." Of course there are no guarantees that the spirits will appear when you are looking for them.

When you are ready to hit the road, take TX 49 about a mile to the east to get out of town. Turn north (left) on FM 248 when you get to the intersection. Almost immediately you'll cross the railroad track, and then you will be on your way, going around curves over gentle hills.

Initially, the hills are almost bumpy, little ones, one after another with curves and a few 90 degree turns. They just keep coming. Three or four separate curves with reduced speed limits in a mile of riding is not an unusual stretch. Then the next mile of road is just as twisty.

The narrow road has a double yellow stripe. The road is too twisty for safe passing, but it makes for fun riding. At various places along the side of the road are signs pointing the way to country cemeteries. These may be the final resting places of those daredevils who tried to pass around the curves. Or maybe they are the homes of the restless souls who are reported to wander in the night.

There are a few houses along the side of the road and alternating forests and pastures off to the side. In some of the pastures there will be cattle and horses grazing. Behind the tall stand of native trees that line the road there may be a shorter forest taking shape. Efforts at re-forestation are ensuring that this area will always have forests. Vultures might be in the middle of the road devouring some yummy road kill, but they are good about getting out of the way of a pack of bikes, or for even one.

The Grove, a private home, may be the most haunted house in Jefferson.

MITCHEL WHITINGTON

About ten miles into the ride, you'll cross another set of railroad tracks. Then the road will continue with twists, turns, and switchbacks. None are too steep or sharp, just constantly coming one after another. Another constant is the sign that warns of possible ice before each bridge. If the temperatures are dropping or have been below freezing, be exceedingly careful.

After about eighteen miles of glorious riding you'll come to a stop sign at the intersection with TX 43. Instead of exploring the community of Bivins, go south (right).

Bivins to Caddo Lake

State highways are different from farm-to-market roads. Nowhere is this more obvious than here. Although TX 43 only has two lanes, it is wider than FM 248 and it has a shoulder. The surface is smoother and there is a painted stripe down the center. When the center stripe is not two double yellow lines it is a single yellow line, indicating that this is a road with long, curvy turns and restricted passing. Here you can run the limit and still enjoy the terrain and beautiful views.

The road goes straight in places, but even those stretches come with gentle hills or long lumpy ones. The mounds follow one another, almost like a roller coaster, one starting before the last one has ended. The mailboxes planted by the side of the road remind bikers that this is a rural area where houses and facilities are far apart.

Turn left onto FM 2198 to go to Uncertain. One story about how the town got its name is that when the city fathers went to register the town they still had not decided among themselves what it should be called. So they put "uncertain" in the blank for the town's name. The name then became official.

One thing is certain, you will enjoy your sojourn through Uncertain. The flea market is always an interesting place to stop, especially if there is a chili cook-off. Just past the flea market shed, the road makes a sharp turn to the left.

Stop just down the road at the Caddo Grocery. You can get corn bread mix, cold drinks, hot links, fishing license, ice, and tours of the lake at this full-service grocery. The barbeque sandwiches are among the best you'll ever eat, especially at the price.

All along the narrow road are fishing camps, RV parks, and small motels, all built right up to the water's edge. Cypress knolls amble into the swampy waters, distorting the shoreline. Spanish moss hangs heavy from the trees, reaching down to brush the necks of wanderers. Another thing that's certain: This is spooky.

County Road 2415 loops through town. As on all county roads, you must watch for potholes and other hazards. Continue on and after about two miles the road connects with FM 2198. Turn right to backtrack, and take the curves from the opposite direction.

When you get to the intersection with TX 43, continue straight. You'll now be going north on FM 134. The road provides more good riding for the next twelve miles back to Jefferson. The two lanes look like a rippled ribbon, with one hill coming immediately after the one before. There are enough curves so the center stripe is either double yellow or at least a single yellow line on one side or the other. Trees and pastures beside of the road make this a truly beautiful area to ride through.

At the fork in the road, go right on US 59 B/TX 134. Right after you cross the Big Cypress Bayou you will enter Jefferson. You can stop and enjoy the town or you can continue straight to the junction with TX 49 going west (left). Since Jefferson has a population of only 2,199, getting through town is a simple matter.

TX 49 starts with four lanes, but narrows to two in about a mile. In another two miles head towards the Lake O' the Pines by turning left onto FM 729. Long white fences stretch along the side of the two-lane road, creating a pastoral vista. The roadside is not as forested here as it was on the first leg of this ride. The rural countryside still sports long hills and lots of easy curves. Frequent passing lanes help you get around anyone going too slow.

There are a number of bridges over various creeks that empty into the lake. Some creeks, such as Hurricane Creek and Johnson Creek, look more like rivers than creeks. Enjoy the view from the bridge, regardless of the name. All along this road you'll see signs announcing US Army Corps of Engineers parks off to the left. Take any of these exits to ride to the banks of the lake.

Stretches of FM 729 have one curve after another with reduced speed limits, sometimes three or four in the space of a mile. Rolling hills add to the fun of taking the curves.

About a mile after a 90-degree curve you will come to a stop sign at a red blinking light, marking the intersection with TX 155. Turn right to go to Avinger. For the next seven miles the road switches back

Bikes parked in front of Auntie Skinner's are a typical weekend sight in Jefferson.

and forth between two and four lanes. When it only has two lanes, it has a double yellow stripe down the center. Stretches of state highways with very little traffic, like this one, are ideal for motorcycles.

If you're hungry when you get to Avinger, population 454, turn left to go into the business district. The 5D Cattle Company and Steak House has the reputation of being one of the best places in the area for beef. Otherwise, turn right onto TX 49 to head back to Jefferson.

These last eighteen miles provide first-rate riding. With hills, curves, and gorgeous wildflowers in the spring, what more could you ask for?

Highlights Along the Way

Jefferson.
   Auntie Skinner's Riverboat Club & Restaurant. This is a popular restaurant with bikers and locals. Live entertainment on weekend nights. 107 W. Austin St. 903/665-7121.
   Ghosts have been reported at the following locations in Jefferson:
   Hotel Jefferson and Lamachio's Restaurant, 124 W. Austin St. 903/665-6177, www.hotel-jefferson.com.
   Falling Leaves Bed and Breakfast. 304 E. Jefferson St. 903/665-8803, www.fallingleavesinn.com.
   Lamacheo's Italian Restaurant. 124 W. Austin St. 903/665-6177, www.lamache.com.
   Big Cypress Coffee House. 123 W. Austin St. 903/665-6655.
   The Grove. 405 Moseley St. 903/665-8018, thegrove-jefferson.com.

Hill Country

Ask any biker who has been around for awhile about his/her favorite ride and you will get the same answer. Everyone's favorite is somewhere in the Texas Hill Country.

Just the name for Central Texas, the Hill Country, tells you that this region is filled with hills, not towering mountains as in West Texas nor flat plains as along the coast, but steep hills with roads that go up and down and curves that swirl around and back. The hills require skill to navigate, partly because of the rugged terrain that follows natural geological formations and partly because of the incredible beauty that can overwhelm and distract even the most experienced rider.

In the spring, blankets of native wildflowers carpet the hills in an array of colors a rainbow would envy. At any time of the year, the cedar- and cactus-studded hills rise in the distance, beyond valleys dipping sharply below the roadbed. Each twist and turn of the road and each crest of a hill reveals an even more stunning view than the curve before. Scatter in a few lakes; clean, fresh-water rivers; a healthy dose of history; and a relaxed, laid-back atmosphere, and you understand why everyone loves to ride in the geographical center of the state.

Take any farm-to-market or ranch road outside of Austin, San Antonio, Kerrville, or surroundings, and you will be in the middle of the best scenery and the best, most interesting riding anywhere. You can't go wrong. Those who have ridden the Hill Country have personal favorites; everyone else wants to experience them.

A lot of the roads are steep, with sharp turns that go on for miles. For example, Lime Creek Road just outside of Volente is an experienced biker's dream. It is the road fantasies are made of for those with skill and confidence. For the less experienced rider and families this road may be too much, but the more you ride on the great Hill Country roads the more ready you will become to try the routes the big boys ride. But even those who are not ready to venture into the big leagues can enjoy the riding here. Most roads do not present death-defying challenges, but, rather, fun with extravagant views of mountains, valleys and wildflowers.

The early immigrants to this area knew a good thing when they saw it. In fact, a number of utopian communities were attempted in this area. It's not hard to understand why nineteenth-century intellectuals wanted to contemplate the world in a place where you can look out over miles and miles of virgin territory and marvel at the wonders of the universe.

Ride 13: Hill Country Adventure
Volente, Marble Falls, Johnson City, Dripping Springs

No matter where you are from or wherever else you ride in the entire world, at some point you have to experience the roads in the Hill Country Adventure Ride. This ride begins near the legendary Lime Creek Road, which many consider to provide some of the best riding in the state. The best way to get there is on RR 2769, which challenges even the cockiest rider with steep hills and sharp curves that slip through canopies of trees and glide along rugged ridges. For mile after mile the hairpin turns and 90-degree switchbacks follow one after another in rapid succession on a narrow two-lane road.

If you're not up for some challenging riding, skip RR 2769 to the village of Volente and Lime Creek Road on the way to Cedar Park. Instead, take US 183 and begin the ride in Cedar Park. The rest of the ride goes through some of the beautiful Texas Hill Country that is as rich in history as it is in first-class, but not as dodgy, riding. Following this route will take you through the homeland of Lyndon B. Johnson— Johnson City and the area around the Pedernales River. You'll pass wineries, a grotto, peach and vegetable stands, and see grazing sheep and longhorns.

If you want an exciting adventure ride plus assurance that you can get back to where you started, start from the beginning, kick back, and have fun.

Getting Started: Ranch Road 620 to Volente

The symbol RR originally denoted a Ranch Road that connected isolated areas with markets. RR 620 may have done this once upon a time, but now the area is rapidly falling victim to urban sprawl. What

Ride 13: Hill Country Adventure
Volente, Marble Falls, Johnson City, Dripping Springs

Getting to Volente from

Austin–25 miles
Corpus Christi–241 miles
Fort Worth–184 miles
Houston–184 miles
Lakeway–18 miles
San Antonio–103 miles

The Ride, 121 miles

RR 620 to Volente
West on RR 2769 (6 miles)

Volente to Cedar Park
Right on Lime Creek Road (6 miles)

Cedar Park to Marble Falls
West (left) on RR 1431 (30 miles)

Marble Falls to Johnson City
South (left) on US 281 (23 miles)

Johnson City to Dripping Springs
East (left) on RR 2766 (10 miles)
South (right) on RR 3232 (9 miles)
East (left) on US 290 (9 miles)

Dripping Springs to RR 620 and RR 2769
North on RR 3238 (14 miles)
East (right) on TX 71 (1 mile)
North (left) on RR 620 (13 miles)

was once way out in the middle of nowhere now shelters a growing population trying to get away from the hustle and bustle of city life. Even multiple lanes in each direction get congested at times. Fortunately, taking the exit to Volente at the intersection of RR 620 and FM 2769 gets you out of the traffic almost immediately.

You'll see a sign that warns of sharp turns and steep grades for the next six miles; that is exactly what you will experience on one of the best motorcycle roads anywhere. Take it slow, especially if you are not an expert. And if you are an expert, you know that you have to pay close attention to this kind of riding. Don't even think about riding without a helmet.

One of the first places you'll notice as you leave the more populated corridor along the road to Volente is a tombstone store. Whatever you want in the way of a cemetery headstone is available here. Take this ride carefully so your kin won't have to stop here to make a purchase.

After that grisly reminder of what can happen if you ditch the helmet, the fun begins. Corkscrew turns, one after another, all under a canopy of trees, make this one of the most thrilling and beautifully enchanting six-mile stretches you will ever ride. The scenery is rugged, with trees on both sides of the road. In places, where the branches form canopies over the roadway, you feel as if you are zooming through a natural green tunnel. Occasionally, bits of lake peek though the trees to the left and then disappear behind the branches until the next clearing a little farther down the road.

The riding is a combination of everything steep, sharp, and exhilarating. As tempting as it is to let your

Be on the lookout for shady curves near Volente.

eyes and mind wander to enjoy the vistas of valleys and trees all around you, pay close attention to the road. One sign after another gives lowered speed limits for upcoming curves: 35 mph, 30 mph, 40 mph, 20 mph, even 15 mph. The lower the speed limit the sharper the curve or the longer the series of curves. Signs warn of particularly sharp curves with 90-degree angles and twisty corkscrews that keep coming and switching back and forth. The stretches between the signs may also be curvy and twisty even if there is no imminent signage. Other signs will remind you that certain areas may flood and that some bridges are narrow. Just remember that there is a good reason for both kinds of signs, and you need to heed the warnings.

Don't be intimidated by the cyclists you might pass. Remember, this is Lance Armstrong country.

You'll pass the Anderson Grist Mill and Museum. The mill was built in the 1860s and displays memorabilia of the area. At Volente Beach Park enjoy the swimming, water slides, and volleyball. Take a sharp right turn onto Lime Creek Road. A sign points the way, but you have to turn right regardless, because that's the way the road turns. Lime Creek Road is six miles filled with very technical, tight, decreasing radius turns, on hills that amplify the adventure.

Volente to Cedar Park

Follow the sign to Cedar Park after you take a dip in Lake Travis. Up ahead there are still twisty curves where hairpin turns switch back and forth on inclines. The grade is not quite as steep as the preceding six miles, but the curves keep coming, one after another. The next one begins before the last one ends, then the road switches back in the other direction on another curve. This is a biker's paradise, the road you live to ride if you want to claim that you have ridden Texas.

As you approach Cedar Park the road straightens out a bit, but the sights are still beautiful. Now you'll be able to pay a little bit more attention to your surroundings.

When you get to Cedar Park, you can step back almost a century and ride on vintage train pulled by the Hill Country Flyer, a 1916 steam locomotive.

Cedar Park to Marble Falls

As you might expect, there are a lot of cedar trees in the Cedar Park vicinity. When you get to the stop sign at West Whitestone Boulevard, turn left. This is RR 1431, the way to Marble Falls. If you have to cut the ride short, take a right instead to zip back to RR 620, just a bit farther north from where you turned off to Volente.

Although it starts as a four-lane highway with a turning lane in the middle, this soon goes back to being a two-lane country road. Curves and hills are much calmer than the stretch you just finished, but you'll still enjoy the moderate challenge. Lago Vista greets you with beautiful long sweeping hills and curves. A little farther down the road you'll see some incredible hilltop mansions. Don't gawk too much. Remember that the dudes living there are wishing they were you out on your bike.

You'll pass through the Balcones Canyon Wildlife Refuge, so watch for critters that might venture out onto the road, not realizing the hazard they present to themselves as well as to you. During wildflower season this is a spectacular run. Even when the flowers are not in bloom you'll get a glorious view of the Hill Country each time you crest a mound. Vistas like these, coupled with steep curves and an occasional low-water crossing, are why the Hill Country is so many bikers' favorite region.

Marble Falls got its name from the Colorado River falling over marble. The area is famous for the beautiful pink and red marble quarried here. In addition to Buchanan, Inks, Lyndon B. Johnson, Marble Falls, and Travis lakes, and all the water activities they have to offer, the area also offers food, fuel, and lodging. For good homemade chow, turn left at the light onto US 281 and stop at the Bluebonnet Cafe. It has been around for a long time. The number of cars and bikes in the parking lot and the taste of the food indicate that it will be around for a long time to come. Save room for pie.

Marble Falls to Johnson City

As you leave Marble Falls on US 281, take a detour through the windy road to Horseshoe Bay for an informal tour through streets of incredible homes. You've heard about it so now's your chance to see it, and you might even make some of those rich folks jealous because you are on a bike and they are not.

The road to Johnson City, US 281, has four lanes and a turning lane. Now you can kick back and relax on the gentle hills and curves. You deserve a chance to become one with your bike and cruise.

The farther south you go, the gentler and flatter the road. Enjoy the tame journey through the serene pasture lands. Stop for peaches at a roadside stand. Don't be surprised if you see wild turkeys and deer.

Johnson City to Dripping Springs

As you get closer to Johnson City you'll experience more hills and more gorgeous views. Cross the famous Pedernales River, which flows through LBJ's ranch and becomes Lake Travis in Austin. Take a right at the sign pointing the way to the LBJ Boyhood Home and Historical Park, two blocks south (right) on US 290. In addition to the 1920s-era frame house, there is also a visitor's center and an old ranch complex once owned by the president's grandfather and uncle.

US 290 continues to Fredericksburg, the starting point for two other Hill Country rides—Heart of the Hill Country and Nowhere but

Luckenbach. You can continue past the fourteen miles down US 290 to connect up with one of the other rides.

Or you can continue this route without making any of these detours and take the left exit to Pedernales Falls State Park on RR 2766. On the way to the park, dips and curves make for more exhilarating

Heed the Winding Road warning at the endtrance to Pedernales State Park.

riding. Watch for flooding. Part of the river through the park is open for tubing, a popular activity in this area and something everyone needs to try at least once. If you don't do it here, do it somewhere else while you're in the Hill Country.

You'll pass the Texas Hills Vineyard. As always, be careful if you decide to stop to sample the goods.

Ten miles beyond Johnson City is Pedernales Falls State Park. At the entrance a sign says "Windy Road, 3 miles." Take this detour, not just for what you see but also for the good riding on the way there. The falls are created by a clear, spring-fed river flowing down gently sloping limestone.

Once you turn right onto RR 3232 the hills pick up again. This is ranchland with more longhorns, goats, and oak trees than people. If you blink when you go through Henley, you'll miss it. Keep on past the New Canaan Farms, where local jams, jellies, and salsas are made. It features a 1900 vintage kitchen and the large oak tree where Lyndon Johnson made his first political speech when he was only twenty-two. Continue on to Dripping Springs, where the most recent "Alamo" was filmed. Unfortunately, the set is on private property and you can't see it from the road. Ride on by and imagine a grimy band of Texians bravely holding off the army from the south.

Dripping Springs to Ranch Road 620 to Ranch Road 2769

Wildflour Bakery offers whole grain bread and other nutritious and delicious treats. Or go down a little farther into town, where you will find additional establishments that welcome bikers.

To get out of Dripping Springs, take a jog on FM 12 to get to RR3238. Turn right unless you want a cool diversion. Then, when you come to RR 3238, follow the signs to Hamilton Pool. This is a Travis County preserve, "Yours to Enjoy Naturally," according to the greeting on the entrance sign. Hamilton Pool's grotto and waterfall make it a cool, refreshing stop. Turn around after your detour to continue on this route

You'll enjoy a pleasant ride with some good hills and curves. The closer you get to Austin, the hillier and curvier the road gets. TX 71, which can be busy during peak times of the day, is one of those rare highways that provides pleasurable riding.

Once you turn left on RR 620 you'll know you're close to where you began this ride, because you will see more cars and more commercial areas. However, you'll still have some superb views and thrilling stretches before the end of the journey. You won't be the only biker out here, for this is motorcycle heaven.

Highlights Along the Way

Anderson Grist Mill and Museum. Memorabilia on area history and an 1860 mill. 13974 FM 2769.

Volente Beach Park: Five-acre water park on Lake Travis. Swimming, sandy beaches, volleyball areas, 40-foot water slides, children's area, basketball court, restaurant. 16197 FM 2769. 512/258-5109, www.volentebeach.com.

Hill Country Flyer. 1916 steam locomotive train departing from Cedar Park on weekends. 512/477-8468, www.austinsteamtrain.org.

Marble Falls. Visitors Center in the century-old railroad depot. 800/759-8178, www.marblefalls.org.
    Bluebonnet Cafe. Friendly home cooking. 211 Hwy. 281. 830/693-2344, www.bluebonnetcafe.net.

LBJ Boyhood Home and Historical Area. Guided tours of the 100-year-old boyhood home of the 36th president, restored to the 1920s. One block away is the old ranch complex called Johnson Settlement, once owned by LBJ's grandfather and uncle. Includes an 1856 dogtrot cabin, 1880 stone farm buildings, exhibit center, longhorn cattle. Visitors Center with information, exhibits, unique audio/visual programs, and ranger talks. Johnson City. 830/868-7128, www.nps.gov/lyjo/boyhood.htm.

Pedernales Falls State Park. Nearly 5,000 acres of preserved natural beauty, including spring-fed waterfalls and abundant wildlife. Parts of the river are open to wading, tubing, swimming, and fishing. Also hiking and camping. FM 2766, about 8 miles east of Johnson City. 800/792-1112 or 830-868-7304, www.tpwd.state.tx.us/park/pedernal/pedernal.htm.

Texas Hills Vineyard. Soil similar to that in Tuscany. Winery tours and tasting room. 830/868-2321, www.texashillsvineyard.com.

New Canaan Farms: Locally made jams, jellies, and salsas. Complex includes a turn-of-the-century kitchen and the large oak tree where Lyndon B. Johnson made his first political speech when he was twenty-two. On US 290 near Dripping Springs. 512/858-7669.

Wildflour Bakery. Natural grains bakery. 2201 W. Highway 290. 512/858-5037.

Hamilton Pool. Beautiful natural area with grotto and waterfall. FM 3238. 512/264-2740, www.texasoutside.com/hamiltonpool.htm.

Ride 14: The Devil's Backbone
San Marcos, Canyon Lake, and Wimberley

This route goes through areas with hellacious names, but the riding is pure heaven. Starting in San Marcos, named by Franciscan friars, the Devil's Backbone ride alternates between heaven and hell. With side trips to Canyon Lake and down Purgatory Road, you'll experience great riding at both ends of the celestial cycle.

No matter where you ride in Central Texas, you'll encounter roads with hills, curves, and extraordinary scenery. The Devil's Backbone is a winding, razor-sharp ridge overlooking vast expanses of Texas Hill Country. This ride follows part of the Backbone and then ventures into tamer territory. You get a sample of adventure as well as some less demanding stretches of first-class riding.

People around here tend to be laid back, accepting, and open minded. Maybe this results from all the intellectuals at the universities, especially the University of Texas in Austin and LBJ's alma mater, Texas State University in San Marcos. Or maybe it's a holdover from the early settlers who came here from the old country. Most came to farm, ranch, and seek their fortunes. Some came to create utopian communities, all of which failed. Along with the incredible riding, you'll also encounter incredible people wherever you happen to stop.

Getting Started: San Marcos and the Devil's Backbone

San Marcos, named for Saint Mark, is the perfect place to take off for the Devil's Backbone. You might want to take a quick tour of Texas

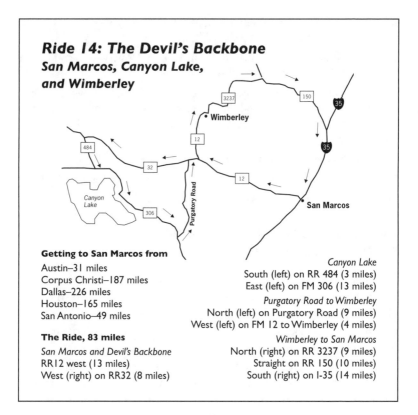

Ride 14: The Devil's Backbone
San Marcos, Canyon Lake, and Wimberley

Getting to San Marcos from
Austin–31 miles
Corpus Christi–187 miles
Dallas–226 miles
Houston–165 miles
San Antonio–49 miles

The Ride, 83 miles
San Marcos and Devil's Backbone
RR12 west (13 miles)
West (right) on RR32 (8 miles)

Canyon Lake
South (left) on RR 484 (3 miles)
East (left) on FM 306 (13 miles)
Purgatory Road to Wimberley
North (left) on Purgatory Road (9 miles)
West (left) on FM 12 to Wimberley (4 miles)
Wimberley to San Marcos
North (right) on RR 3237 (9 miles)
Straight on RR 150 (10 miles)
South (right) on I-35 (14 miles)

State University, formerly Southwest Texas State, the alma mater of Lyndon Johnson; Aquarena Center, an educational and scientific center focusing on the Edwards Aquifer; Wonder World, built around a natural cavern formed by an earthquake; or Prime and Tanger outlets, a huge shopping complex just north of town.

Fortunately, RR 12, which intersects the Devil's Backbone, crosses the major highway through town, I-35. Take the exit west toward Wimberley. For a half-mile or so, RR 12 meanders through town, past shops and places to eat. After you cross the San Marcos River you will see fewer and fewer commercial establishments. Take a right on Moore Street, which is RR 12 and part of the Texas Hill Country Trail. From this point on you will be traveling up and down hills that begin even before you get out of the city limits. Each thrill and view surpasses the one before.

A sign announcing a corkscrew curve with a speed of 25 mph short-ly after leaving the city limits of San Marcos is just the beginning. The road initially has two lanes plus a passing lane. After a while the passing lane disappears, and the ubiquitous double yellow stripe appears. With all the curves, hills, and limited sight, this is not a good place to chance a slip into the lane of oncoming traffic for passing. Instead, relax and savor the road.

Hills, curves, and great scenery make riding in the Hill Country out of this world. The hills come one after another. Before you finish one, the next begins, like a roller coaster higher and lower, then around and up again. In the dips and declines, occasional signs warn of water on the roads, an important piece of information if there've been recent rains.

The regular speed limit here is 60 mph, reasonable for the riding conditions during the usually clear weather. There are only a few cross streets, but there is so much more to look at. In places, trees line both sides of the road, making you feel as if you are riding through a can-yon of forests. Deer are plentiful; you might actually see one wandering around on the side of the road or even trying to cross in front of you. Some years there are so many that they are downright dangerous. A doe or a buck may not be as big as an elephant, but hitting one would cer-tainly feel like it was. This is a big hunting area, so do not take a chance by going into posted areas.

After about six miles, this heavenly, hilly road takes a sharp turn to the left. Still two lanes wide with a small shoulder, the road now allows passing. Even though the hills are a little flatter, there are still lots of mild curves with the regular speed limit.

About four miles past the sharp left, ride straight through the blinker on RR 32 as if going to Blanco. Another option is to continue on RR 12 toward Wimberley and then back home. Both routes give great riding, one just gives more of it.

The long curves and hills on RR 32 are a calmer version of the more vigorous RR 12. You can get on some speed as you zoom by goats lazily grazing in the roadside pastures. Finally, you'll see a sign that says "Devil's Backbone." You are on the winding ridge route that you have heard all your biker buddies rave about. The riding and views are phe-nomenal, and just keep improving.

The road has two lanes and wide shoulders as the ridge curves and climbs along a path carved out of the mountains. About five miles into the Backbone there is a picnic area at a scenic overlook. Stop to stare into the valleys below and the mountains beyond and contemplate the wonders and miracles that made this ride possible. The road demands your attention, so this is your best chance to soak up the scenery.

You'll see only a few houses, because this is ranching country. Trees grow in thick stands on the side of the road. Deer and falling rocks are two hazards to watch out for; either one can suddenly appear.

Continue on RR 32 all the way to Blanco to ride the full length of the Devil's Backbone and to relish more fabulous riding along the natural ridge. Once you get to Blanco, turn around and experience it from a different direction, or take US 290 through Dripping Springs and back to I-35, about 47 miles.

Canyon Lake

For a taste of different but still magnificent Hill Country riding, after eight miles of riding the Backbone on RR 32 turn left at RR 484 toward Canyon Lake. Immediately, you will be on a very good hill with a curve. Turn left on FM 306. Here you'll traverse long, rolling hills and curves with stunning views as you head toward Canyon Lake City, about ten miles ahead. Once again you'll zip around corkscrews as the altitude declines. Not surprisingly, the two-lane road has a double yellow stripe down the center; this is no place to pass. If you get a chance, glance into the distance; the views are awesome, especially at the crests of the hills.

To get up close and personal with the lake, turn into Canyon Park at the US Army Corps of Engineers sign. Here you'll find beach, swimming, group shelter, picnicking, camping, and hiking. While in the park, watch out for the hills and curves; there may be rocks on the roads.

Once you get back to FM 306, take a right. You will encounter even more hills and curves. This road has two lanes with a double yellow stripe and a good shoulder. Canyon City's eating establishments include good places that are not part of national chains, such as Roy's Seafood and Steak. For a different type of adventure, try tubing down the Guadalupe River. There are a number of places to rent a tube or a raft.

Purgatory

About two miles after you see a sign that tells you I-35 is thirteen miles ahead, you will come to Purgatory Road. Turn left. Get ready for a desolate adventure through a part of the Hill Country only those with "local knowledge" ever trek.

A 20 mph curve greets you with a taste of what's to come. The two-lane road has no shoulder and is subject to flooding. The double yellow stripe warns you not to pass, but, then, you may not see another vehicle on the road. Signs warn of limited sight distance, but you can already

see that. This is definitely rural riding, through isolated pastures complete with a couple of cattle guards and a very narrow bridge. What makes this road purgatory is not hellacious riding but, rather, the rocky desolation. At the stop sign at the dead end of Purgatory Road, turn right. Take a left to

Rocks strewn by nature add to the desolate appearance along Purgatory Road.

Wimberley at the intersection with RR 12. Or, if you are ready to head on back, turn right toward San Marcos. After four miles of curves, corkscrews, and great views, Wimberley pops out at you.

Wimberley to San Marcos

Wimberley is a quaint town of nearly 4,000 people, many of them artists, writers, and musicians. It was named as one of America's Ten Best Small Towns by Travel Holiday magazine. You'll understand why when you visit. The whole area is chock-full of fun shops, B & B's, and great restaurants.

There are a number of ways to get out of town and back to the beginning of the ride. Leave town on RR 3237 and continue straight on RR 150 all the way to I 35. Turn south (right) to go back to San Marcos or north (left) to head toward Austin. If you end up loitering in Wimberley longer than anticipated, head east (right) on RR 12 to hotfoot it back to San Marcos. It's only about fourteen miles away.

Or you can head North on RR 12 for eleven miles of sharp curves with reduced mileage, corkscrews, and more regular curves. You'll weave past Driftwood Vineyards. In Dripping Springs, RR 12 crosses US 290. Take a right to head back to I 35. At I-35 turn south (right) to go back to San Marcos, or stay on the interstate to go to your original starting point. Following this route, Wimberley is about forty-four miles to San Marcos

Whichever way back you choose, you will have to admit that riding the Devil's Backbone and the surrounding area is devilishly good fun.

Highlights Along the Way

San Marcos. www.ci.san-marcos.tx.us.

Texas State University. Lyndon Johnson's alma mater. 601 University Dr. 512/245-2111, www.txstate.edu.

Aquarena Center. Educational and scientific center focusing on the Edwards Aquifer. Glass-bottom boat tours. 921 Aquarena Springs Dr., 512/245-7570. www.aquarena.txstate.edu.

Wonder World. Entertainment complex around natural cavern formed by an earthquake. 512/392-3760, www.wonderworldpark.com.

Discount shopping: Prime Outlets, 3939 S. IH-35, 512/396-2200; Tanger Factory Outlets, 4015 S IH-35, 512/396-7446.

Canyon Park. One of several on Canyon Lake. Wildtexas.com/parks/canyon. php.

Wimberley. www.wimberleyonline.com.

Driftwood Vineyards. 21550 Ranch Road 12, Driftwood. 512/858-4508. www. driftwoodvineyards.com.

Ride 15: Thrills and Beauty in the Hill Country
Fredericksburg to Kerrville and Back

Getting to Fredericksburg, the starting point of this ride, will whet your appetite for the thrills and beauty to come. No matter which route you chose, you will ride along fantastic ridges, around sharp curves, and over superb hills. The most common route to Fredericksburg is US 290 through Johnson City.

Traveling from Johnson City to Fredericksburg is thirty-one miles of riding bliss on four lanes of gentle curves. In the spring, this area is blanketed with the beautiful state flower, the bluebonnet, as well as with all sorts of other varieties of wildflowers. Lyndon Johnson's Lady Bird loved these wildflowers, and you will be as overwhelmed by their beauty as she was. For some wildflower seeds to take back home you can stop at Wildseed Farms, the largest working wildflower farm in the country, about seven miles before you get to Fredericksburg.

A number of the Texas wineries along this route give tours and have tasting rooms. Stop and taste all you want. Just do it the official way—taste but don't swallow. A list of some of the wineries open to the public appears in the Highlights section of this ride.

In season you will pass fresh fruit and vegetable stands along the way. Stonewall, named for Confederate Gen. "Stonewall" Jackson, now attributes its fame to the tasty peaches grown in the region. They are juicy and sweet and worth a stop to buy some.

The Lyndon B. Johnson National Historical Park and the LBJ State Park and Historic Site are next to each other about thirteen miles out of Johnson City in Stonewall. Board the bus for the tour of the 600-acre LBJ Ranch at the state park. A bus tour will take you by Johnson's Texas White House and his final resting site. Both state and national areas have a number of restored historical buildings, white-tailed deer, buffalo, and Texas Longhorns—the cattle variety, not the university kind. The state park area also has picnicking, a swimming pool, and a nature trail.

The Old Tunnel Wildlife Management Area, just before you get to Fredericksburg, is a fascinating place to go around dusk. Two million Mexican free-tailed bats emerge from an abandoned railway tunnel.

Once you finally get to Fredericksburg, you may be tempted to make this the end of the journey. Many bikers and other tourists consider Fredericksburg their final destination. If you do that you might not ride out of town until your third or fourth trip here.

Fredericksburg is a peaceful town, and always has been. When the Germans originally settled here, this was Comanche territory. Of course, the natives did not particularly like the intruders, but they negotiated a lasting peace. Unlike most treaties between settlers and Indians, neither side ever broke the agreement.

Today the German influence is still strongly felt, not only in the architecture of historical landmarks but also in the food, atmosphere, and celebrations of the town. You will feel the influence of the Europeans who settled here along the entire ride from Fredericksburg to Kerrville and back.

Anyone who enjoys the outdoors will love this part of the Hill Country. Hunters come because something is almost always in season. Bicyclists and bikers both gather here. All these special interest groups know this is a worthy destination as well as a fun stop along the way.

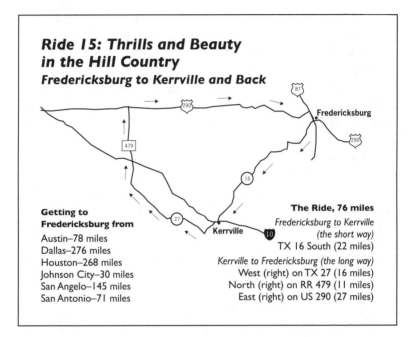

Ride 15: Thrills and Beauty in the Hill Country
Fredericksburg to Kerrville and Back

Getting to Fredericksburg from

Austin–78 miles
Dallas–276 miles
Houston–268 miles
Johnson City–30 miles
San Angelo–145 miles
San Antonio–71 miles

The Ride, 76 miles

Fredericksburg to Kerrville
(the short way)
TX 16 South (22 miles)
Kerrville to Fredericksburg (the long way)
West (right) on TX 27 (16 miles)
North (right) on RR 479 (11 miles)
East (right) on US 290 (27 miles)

Getting Started: Fredericksburg to Kerrville (the short way)

Don't be surprised if the four lanes of US 290 get a bit congested on weekends, especially if there is one of the frequent festivals. For a town of less than 9,000 people there's often a disproportionate number of tourists here. Because it's such a small town, you can park your bike in one of the on-street spaces or in one of the free lots around town and walk anywhere you want to go.

Fredericksburg has great pride in its heritage and its beautiful surroundings. The folks who live here love visitors, no matter how they arrive, and want you to have a good time.

Wherever you walk you'll pass tempting restaurants, quaint bed and breakfasts, and intriguing shops. In fact, more than three hundred homes and buildings have been converted into B & B's or guesthouses. Plus there are the typical chain motels. Maps and guides are plentiful and readily available.

In the early days, families from surrounding areas would come into town on the weekends so they could attend church on Sunday. Many built small houses, called Sunday Houses, to stay in on Saturday night.

One interesting spot is the Admiral Nimitz State Historic Site and National Museum of the Pacific War. There are buildings and exhibits of local interest in addition to the military museum that houses, among other things, life-size exhibits from battles during the Pacific War and the story of Admiral Chester Nimitz, who was born in Fredericksburg.

When you want to hit the road again, turn onto South Adams Street, also TX 16, the road to Kerrville. After just a few lights, you are out of town and riding on long, gentle curves. Occasionally the two-lane road with wide shoulders curves sharply as it passes ranches, pastures, and a little cropland. Small, rolling hills give way to some of the area's most overwhelmingly beautiful scenery. Curves and hills create an ever-changing viewpoint for vistas

Distant farmers built Sunday Houses in Fredericksburg so they could spend Saturday night in town before attending church.

in every direction. Not only are the views stunning, the riding is also.

As you approach Kerrville, you'll see the sign to Scenic Hills Road, a twisty, curvy loop of about three miles into the hills. The narrow road with no shoulder climbs steeply and curves. Corkscrew turns with speed limits of 20 to 30 mph take you to the top and down again. At the dead end, turn right onto Scenic Valley. This takes you through a residential area and back to TX 16. Only expert riders need attempt this detour.

Like Fredericksburg, Kerrville is a town with a predominantly German influence. Unlike Fredericksburg, Kerrville has more millionaires per capita than any other American city except Los Angeles. It only takes thirty seconds in this town to understand why people like it so much. It is beautiful and peaceful, with an appealing quality of life and almost perfect weather.

Kerrville to Fredericksburg (the long way)

Before heading back to Fredericksburg, this ride is going to continue westward for a while. So fuel up and head out.

The easiest way to go west is to take I-10 until it crosses US 290, a logical route heading back east. But if you want to ride the real Texas and experience some more of the rural Hill Country terrain, go through town until you get to the intersection of TX 16 and TX 27. Go west (right) toward Ingram. A road with two lanes and a shoulder will take you over more hills and around more curves to Ingram, only six miles away.

A good detour out of Ingram is TX 39 toward Hunt. More hills and curves take you to Stonehenge in the Hills, a sixty-percent scale model of the famous megaliths of Salisbury, England, sprouting in the Texas Hill Country. There are also Easter Island-type statues here. Go on back to Ingram, and continue on US 27.

If you've ever wondered why so many bikers love the Hill Country, you won't have to wonder any longer. This is out-of-this-world riding. Hills and curves keep coming, each better and more exciting than the one before, not so steep and sharp as to require a skull and crossbones warning but steep enough and sharp enough to be exhilarating, even thrilling. Going up a hill and schussing down the other side past ranches and fruit orchards is awe-inspiring. Some curves come just as the hill is cresting, so you cannot see the top of the hill or the end of the curve. Just as you think you might fall off the face of the earth or head into the wall of a cliff, the road zooms down, and the excitement starts all over again. Interstate highways never offer adrenaline rushes this exciting.

Wild critters roam in the open territory. In the middle of all the exhilaration, keep an eye out for road kill or animals attempting to become road kill by wandering into the middle of the road. Falling rocks present another potential hazard here. Since the road in places was carved out of hillsides, sheer cliffs can rise from the pavement. Rocks sometimes find their way down to meet your tires—not often, but often enough for you to be on the lookout.

A road like this is one you may never want to leave. But turn north (right) on RR 479 to start the journey back to Fredericksburg. Don't expect heavy traffic or passing lanes. The road starts with a series of wiggle curves and the potential for loose livestock. The isolated country road cuts through pastures and follows a twisty stream.

An occasional cattle guard keeps livestock from stampeding you, but crossing one might be a bit uncomfortable if it takes you by surprise. Don't try to make up time here. This stretch is to enjoy at lower speeds.

When this bit of heaven comes to an end at I-10, you have a choice. Turn east (right), taking the fast road back to Kerrville and retracing your steps to Fredericksburg, or continue straight on RR 479 to US 290. Going straight continues the fresh riding pleasure. Curves keep coming, hills form a ribbon in the distance, one loop beginning before the last ends. The two-lane road has a double yellow stripe down the center.

Occasionally, the double yellow stripe gets down to only a single stripe, but still be careful in passing.

At the intersection with US 290, go east (right). Fredericksburg is twenty-seven miles away. The two lanes soon increase to four, plus shoulder. There are still gentle hills and great views of pasture land. Once you get back to Fredericksburg, you can stop and enjoy the town again before heading back to your homeport.

Highlights Along the Way

Wildseed Farms. Wildflower farm. Viewing of wildflowers, seeds for sale. 7 miles east of Fredericksburg on US 290 at 425 Wildflower Hills. 830/990-1393, www.wildseedfarms.com.

Lyndon B. Johnson National Historical Park. Bus tours of the 600-acre ranch along the Pedernales River. LBJ's reconstructed birthplace as well as his final resting place, the Texas White House, and more. West of Johnson City on US 290. 830/868-7128, www.lakesandhills.com/lbjpark.htm.

Lyndon B. Johnson State Park and Historic Site. Boarding point for the national park bus tour. Also visitor center, exhibits, wildlife displays, historic buildings, swimming pool, tennis courts, picnic facilities, nature trail. 800/792-1112, www.tpwd.lstate.tx.us/park.

Old Tunnel Wildlife Management Area. Two million bats emerge from an abandoned railway tunnel around dusk each evening. Viewing deck and tours. 830/238-4487, www.tpwd.state.tx.us/wma.

Fredericksburg. B&Bs listed on www.fredericksburg-texas.com.

Admiral Nimitz State Historic Site—National Museum of the Pacific War. Restored Nimitz Steamboat Hotel, George Bush Gallery of the National Museum of the Pacific War, Garden of Peace, Pacific Combat Zone exhibit, Memorial Wall, Plaza of the Presidents. 304 E. Main St. 830/997-4379, www.nimitz-museum.org.

Wineries.

Bell Mountain. Chardonnays, Rieslings, Pinot Noir. On TX 16, 14 miles north of Fredericksburg at 463 Bell Mountain Rd. 830/685-3297, www.bellmountainwine.com.

Becker Vineyards: French Bordeaux, Rhone and Burgundy varieties. Jenschke Lane, about a mile off US 290 west of Stonewall. 830/644-2681, www. beckervineyards.com.

Chisholm Trail Winery. 2367 Usener Rd., off US 290 nine miles west of Fredericksburg. 830/990-2675, www.chisholmtrailwinery.com.

Fredericksburg Winery. Special rose marking the 150th anniversary of Fredericksburg. One block west of the courthouse in Fredericksburg at 247 W. Main St. 830/990-8747, www.fbgwinery.com.

Grape Creek Vineyard. 4 miles west of Stonewall on US 290. 830/644-2710, www.grapecreek.com.

Oberhof Winery. Sparkling and specialty wines. 1406 S. Hwy. 87. 830/997-8969.

Ride 16: Nowhere but Luckenbach
Fredericksburg, Luckenbach, Sisterdale and Comfort

Not every ride is worth leaving Fredericksburg for. It's such a fun German town where people love their beer, their music, their bikes, that you might be tempted to stay there for as long as your credit limit holds out. But going to Luckenbach is one trek that might make even the most red of the rednecks and the most blue of the bluebloods glad they came.

The German influence, the laid-back atmosphere of the Hill Country, and a combination of the great people, great terrain—great everything—make the Texas Hill Country an area everyone loves. One of the craziest, zaniest places in the entire area is Luckenbach.

This hamlet got its first post office/general store/bar in 1846, and the store has been open for business ever since. A year later, the community hall, now known as the dance hall, was built. Since then, Luckenbach has been a place for revelry and celebration. Like all ethnic communities created by immigrants during the mid-1800s, Luckenbach faced hard times and almost drifted into oblivion, until Hondo Crouch, former swimming champion, actor, and columnist, bought the ten acres of the town. He declared himself the "Clown Prince of Luckenbach" and declared his town "a free state of mind." That pretty much sums up the irreverent attitude that makes it so popular today.

Come by any afternoon or evening, and see musicians jamming under the oak trees in back or around the pot-bellied stove in the bar during the cooler days. Anyone who wants to can bring an instrument and join in the fun. Come by almost any weekend afternoon and you're liable to meet a posse of other bikers who've also made the trek to Luckenbach.

Sisterdale, down the road and only slightly larger than Luckenbach, was one of the utopias that German Freethinkers tried to form in the mid 1800s. Many residents formed one of the German immigrant centers of abolitionism and Unionism before and during the Civil War. The town once had a population as high as 150, but it declined to a low of 25 in the early 1900s. It's grown a little since then, but not so much that you can count on getting much more than a soft drink here.

The next stop on this ride is Comfort, another free-thinking, political activist community of German immigrants settled by renegades from Sisterdale. Many buildings are listed in the National Register of Historic Places. They include Bolshevik Hall and numerous half-timber and Victorian structures. At one time Sisterdale was an international wool and mohair center, home of the "Angora Goat King of the World," Adolph Stieler.

Everywhere you go on this ride you will pass Individuals, with a capital "I". This area was settled by those who had their own ideas about the way things should be, and that spirit lives on.

Couple this ride with the Heaven in the Hill Country Ride, that also commences in Fredericksburg, if you want to cover more territory. After one trip here, you'll be back again.

Getting Started: Fredericksburg to Luckenbach

Occasionally you'll come upon a fantastic US highway that is well maintained and wide yet still has wonderful curves and calm, rolling hills that you can run at the speed limit. US 290 out of Fredericksburg, a major four-lane highway with good shoulders, is one of these. The views of the pine and cedar trees make you want to go on forever. Watch for deer crossing the highway.

Ranch Road 1376 comes almost too soon, but the riding only improves after turning south (right). Like most ranch roads, this one is two lanes with no shoulder and is surrounded by pastures, orchards, and trees. These are the hills, the curves, and the views that you live to ride. In the distance you will see tree-covered mountains staring back at you at eye level or above. Then the road ahead looks as if it's dropping off into a stand of trees, only to curve around into more fantasy riding.

About three miles into RR 1376, you'll see some hand-lettered signs announcing "Luckenbach Downtown." Stop if you want to browse the kitsch, but realize that this is not your destination.

Ride 16: Nowhere but Luckenbach
Fredericksburg, Luckenbach, Sisterdale and Comfort

Getting to Fredericksburg from

Austin–78 miles
Dallas–276 miles
Houston–268 miles
Johnson City–30 miles
San Angelo–145 miles
San Antonio–71 miles

The Ride, 60 miles

Fredericksburg to Luckenbach
US 290 (6 miles)
South (right) on RR 1376 (4 miles)
Luckenbach to Sisterdale
South (right) on RR 1376 (15 miles)
Sisterdale to Comfort
West (right) on RR 473 (12 miles)
Comfort to Fredericksburg
North (right) on US 87 (23 miles)

About a mile down the road, after a zigzag you'll come to a one-lane blacktop road to the right. There may or may not be a sign pointing the way, because the Luckenbach sign disappears almost as soon as a new one is put up. Turn anyway. Trees cover the road, and you may think you have made a wrong turn. Keep going. You'll know when you get there.

The field in front of the post office/general store/bar will probably be filled with bikes, especially if you come on a weekend afternoon. Back under the oak trees will be a variety of musicians jamming away. Everyone is welcome to join in or just listen. Get a longneck at the bar and kick back. If it's a bit too chilly to lounge outside, the jamming moves into the bar where everyone gathers around the pot-bellied stove to suck one back. Even hyper-type A's become mellow here.

Those who come just for the music or camaraderie will not want to leave. However, bikers are a different breed, hearing the call of the open road. Find your way back to RR 1376, hang a right, and continue on to Sisterdale.

Luckenbach to Sisterdale

The biggest problem with the next fifteen miles is that they are only fifteen miles, and this segment of the ride is over too soon. You'll pass the Armadillo Farms Campgrounds. Consider overnighting here if you want to stay at Luckenbach for too much music and too many longnecks.

Then the road becomes one roller coaster hill after another. Like any good coaster, the hills keep coming with curves and twists and more, over and over. When your buddy in front crests a hill it will look as if the bike is free-falling off the face of the earth. As you follow, the road dips back down, turns, and climbs again.

The craggy terrain and steep drop-offs on the side of the road create fantastic vistas of the rugged land. As you check out the road in the distance, clouds may obscure your view. This is God's country.

Signs will warn of dips and possible water in the road, and the double yellow stripe down the center will remind you not to pass. As much fun as this stretch is, ride with caution, especially if there has been rain that may still be flowing through the troughs.

If you ever wondered why the Hill Country is everyone's favorite place to ride, you aren't wondering any more.

The central gathering point in Luckenbach is its post office, established in 1846.

Sisterdale to Comfort

Go west (right) on RR 473 at Sisterdale. Cross the West Sister Creek and you are on your way to Comfort. The two-lane road is subject to flooding. Whenever there is a "dip" sign, look out for water in the road. For a little while the hills and curves are serene and relaxing. Enjoy this short breather until the hills and curves begin again. Signs

There are special places for motorcyle parkin' in Luckenbach.

warn of upcoming corkscrews. As always, the lower the speed limit, the sharper and more adventurous the coming curves.

Stop at the dead end and turn left toward Comfort. For the next six miles the road goes through pastures and fields growing hay, a bit gentler riding than before.

Comfort to Fredericksburg

Coming into Comfort is going to look like coming into a big city, even though its population is just around 1,500. Of course, it is really the existence of I-10 that makes the area seem so developed. You can get on the interstate to speed the sixteen miles to Kerrville. Or you can ride under the interstate and keep going straight towards US 87 to Fredericksburg. The four lanes out of Comfort narrow to two once you are out of town. This US highway rides like a smooth state highway, with gentle curves and hills, not sharp, steep ones. Keep an eye out for deer.

US 87 intersects with US 290 in downtown Fredericksburg. You are back, and now you have a second chance to enjoy being here.

Highlights Along the Way

Fredericksburg. See the Heart of the Hill Country ride for information.

Luckenbach. www.luckenbachtexas.com.

Sisterdale.www.tsha.utexas.edu/handbook/online/articles/view/SS/hns51. html.

Comfort.www.comfort-texas.com.

Ride 17: The Road to Mexico
Castroville to Del Rio

Once upon a time, to go west to El Paso you took the route that ultimately became US 90. It was the best way to avoid torturous mountains, and there were enough cool, clear mountain streams through the rough terrain to keep animals and humans alive. Along the way towns sprouted up just often enough, about every twenty to twenty-five miles, to provide a night's lodging and entertainment, some raucous and some refined.

This historic route takes you from the outskirts of the Texas Hill Country to the beginnings of the desert and the Big Bend region of Texas, giving you a taste of both. You can almost see the apparitions of the ghosts that are said to inhabit these parts, so it's a good idea to stay on the roads and heed the signs about flooding, low-water crossings, and sharp turns. You want to be a renegade cowboy on your bike rather than a restless soul haunting the other rebels riding on.

By the number of Border Patrol vehicles parked along the route, you will still feel like you are in frontier territory. The wild spirit of days past thrives along US 90. As you become one with your bike, you'll not only have the thrill of the ride but you'll also see some great vistas and gain insight as to the tough, lonely days of the early travelers.

Because this is an east-west ride, head out in the morning so the sun will be behind you, and come back in the afternoon. Be sure to take along plenty of water, and, if you travel alone, be sure someone else knows your route and cell phone number. This ride can be continued with the Ride across Time (Ride 18) that goes from Del Rio to Fort Stockton. That ride can then be linked with the other Big Bend Region rides.

Getting Started: **Castroville to Brackettville**

The last thing anyone would expect twenty-five miles west of San Antonio is a little bit of Alsace, but that is exactly what Castroville offers. In the 1840s Henri Castro enticed war-weary immigrants from

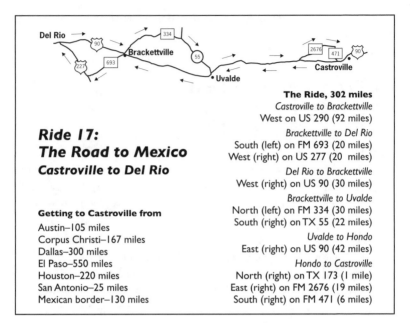

Ride 17:
The Road to Mexico
Castroville to Del Rio

Getting to Castroville from
Austin–105 miles
Corpus Christi–167 miles
Dallas–300 miles
El Paso–550 miles
Houston–220 miles
San Antonio–25 miles
Mexican border–130 miles

The Ride, 302 miles
Castroville to Brackettville
West on US 290 (92 miles)

Brackettville to Del Rio
South (left) on FM 693 (20 miles)
West (right) on US 277 (20 miles)

Del Rio to Brackettville
West (right) on US 90 (30 miles)

Brackettville to Uvalde
North (left) on FM 334 (30 miles)
South (right) on TX 55 (22 miles)

Uvalde to Hondo
East (right) on US 90 (42 miles)

Hondo to Castroville
North (right) on TX 173 (1 mile)
East (right) on FM 2676 (19 miles)
South (right) on FM 471 (6 miles)

Germany, France, Switzerland, and the French-German region of Alsace to come to this West Texas frontier with the promise of free land. Like all immigrants of this period, they tried to recreate a bit of their homeland in their architecture and foods, adapted to the harsh realities of Texas. Although the community thrived for a while, Henri Castro did not prosper. He is credited for introducing more than 2,100 immigrants to Texas, more than any one else other than Stephen F. Austin.

On the way into town you will pass the newest landmark, the Das Haus Aus Elsass or The House from Alsace. This was built in the first half of the sixteen hundreds in Wahlback, France, then disassembled and reassembled in Castroville by university students and artisans from Alsace. Completed and opened to the public in 2002, it houses a plethora of historical household items, all donated and shipped to Castroville from its home region.

The Landmark Inn State Historic Site began as a stagecoach stop. In keeping with its origins, it still accommodates overnight visitors. It also has an interpretive center, water-powered gristmill, and other historical structures and artifacts. It was restored to the 1940s, so there's no television. It does have air conditioning, ceiling fans, and rocking chairs.

Today, many of the area's buildings from the early years remain, some having been converted into private homes or bed and breakfasts. Although the eating establishments now serve typical Tex-Mex and barbeque fare, several Castroville restaurants still offer the fine French cuisine of the first settlers.

The Castroville Chamber of Commerce has an informative visitors guide that is available almost everywhere in the town. It tells you about each of the stops on the walking tour marked by the signs with arrows guiding you to the next landmark. Walking the trail stretches your legs and enables you to enjoy a bit of France in Texas you won't find anywhere else.

When you're ready to take off, head west on US 90 to Hondo. The fifteen-mile stretch of road to Hondo has long, rolling hills that flatten beneath you as you enjoy the wind in your face. The wildflowers sprinkle color along the roadside during the spring, especially if there has been rain.

Across from the H-E-B, Hondo greets you with its city sign that pretty much sums up the sentiments of these parts: "This is God's country. Please don't drive through it like hell."

Good advice. In old Hondo, don't miss Graff's, one-stop shopping for whatever you need, according to the painted signs on the windows. Graff's offers western wear, real estate, cattle, and antiques.

The Medina County Museum is in an 1897 train depot, but there are also other old buildings in the complex. Look for the signs as you pass out of town.

For something a little different, make this trip some weekend between late September and the end of November, so you can attempt to find your way into and out of the South Texas Maze. This giant maze is cut out of a cornfield, and forms patterns visible only from the air. Most people can figure it out in an hour or less, if they can stop laughing long enough to retrace their steps.

The African village for the movie, "Ace Ventura—When Nature Calls" was built on the 777 Exotic Game Ranch just outside Hondo. All sorts of game from Africa, India, and Europe as well as native varieties live here. You can take a safari-style hunt or visit the movie sets.

Next you have nine miles of straight, flat road through open fields. Enjoy the ride, but don't stop. This is a prison area.

D'Hanis is another Alsatian settlement, a bit younger than Castroville, developed to handle the overflow of folks who couldn't get their land grants in the original community. The old stone buildings of "downtown" still stand. Some, like the 1898 J.M. Koch Hotel, are being restored. The hotel, now a B & B, can be seen from US 90, but it is on the other side of the railroad tracks.

During the eleven miles from D'Hanis to Sabinal you'll start to see gradual changes in the scenery. This is a good stretch to let loose and kick back. Enjoy the gentle curves and scenery. Relax and let the bike go.

Good advice in Hondo.

If you don't blink as you go through Knippa, you'll see this sign: "Go ahead and blink, Knippa is bigger than you think."

That's pride!

Uvalde is twenty-two miles down US 90. You can see the mountains in the distance; on the way back you'll see them up close and personal. Uvalde, "Tree City, USA," is the home of former governor Dolph Briscoe and the Garner Memorial Museum and Vice Presidential Library, honoring the infamous "Cactus Jack" Garner, who enjoyed a depression-era reputation for his prowess at whiskey-drinking and poker-playing as well as politics.

Thirty-one miles north of Uvalde on US 83 is Garner State Park. Besides having good riding on the way to the park, once you arrive you can enjoy the tubing, camping, hiking, and the nightly dancing in summer. There's so much to do that if you try to do it all it might make getting to Del Rio the same day a bit tight.

During the next forty miles of the ride you'll notice the road has more curves and hills and that you are climbing in altitude. It's still an easy ride, so you can enjoy the great scenery. Stop at the roadside park if you need a break. The terrain gets more arid, but this is a desert with lots of vegetation.

Brackettville to Del Rio

Just outside Brackettville is Fort Clark Springs, beside the waters of Las Moras Springs, named for the mulberry trees and on the site of the old Fort Clark. Named after a Mexican War hero, the fort was built in the mid-1800s along the military highway from San Antonio to El Paso to help provide safe passage for folks joining the gold rush to California. The first wooden structures were replaced with buildings made from limestone quarried on the site. Barracks built in the 1930s have been converted into a motel. Along with the legally-required posted rates on the inside of the room door is a sign requesting that guests not dress the game shot during hunting in the room. No, this is not a joke. The Old Guardhouse Museum has interesting exhibits on local and pioneer history. Bikers are frequent and welcome guests here. Enjoy the spring-fed swim park that is free and open to the public.

Just outside Brackettville turn left on FM 693. Here the first-rate riding gets even better. You feel as if you are all alone with your bike in the middle of nowhere. There is a good reason for this feeling: you are alone in the middle of nowhere.

The terrain becomes more rugged, and there are a number of sharp, but not hairpin curves. Pay attention to your driving and to the signs by the side of the road. Several warn of water on the road when it rains. A small, overturned boat lies by the side of the road, a shipwreck from a flooded stream, perhaps?

After ten miles of riding through mesquite trees, thorn bushes, an occasional wild aloe plant, and an assortment of Texas cactus, you'll pass a house, the first one since turning off US 90. The curves are challenging enough to be fun, but not dangerous, as long as you pay attention and not get too caught up in the beauty of the vistas.

For a short stretch the road is a bit elevated, so you can look over fields of silvery sage that extend as far as the eye can see. Despite being so isolated, the road is in surprisingly good shape. When it dead-ends at FM 277, turn right. For the next nineteen miles until you reach Del Rio, you will ride on a great road through rugged terrain with impressive, scenic vistas. You might see Border Patrol vans along the way; the men are just doing their job.

One thing you will see a lot of is advertisements and signs to Alamo Village. In spite of the commercialization, this location of the 1959 John Wayne movie is a fascinating place to visit. The Alamo and a complete 1800s frontier village were constructed for the film. In summer there are shows and an occasional shoot-out. In the off-season the buildings are often used to store hay, because this is a working ranch.

Del Rio to Brackettville

When you get to Del Rio, you can take a detour and go into Mexico. Or you can continue with the Ride Through Time (Ride 18) on US 90 to Seminole Canyon State Park and Historic Site about 45 miles further down. There you can view 4,000-year-old cave paintings made by the Seminole Indians. A bit further, in Langtry, you can visit the haunts of the famous Judge Roy Bean, who may have named his town after the famous actress Lily Langtry. That ride continues north to Fort Stockton and is the launching pad for some great West Texas trekking.

Or you can hook a right and head back to Brackettville on US 90. This is a fast, efficient route, but not nearly as much fun as the diversion you just completed. If you want to spend a little time in Del Rio, check out the Ride through Time for highlights of the area.

Brackettville to Uvalde

At Brackettville, turn left at FM 334. You'll pass buildings constructed of locally quarried stone, a school, and some small-town residential areas. Soon you'll be out of town and back into the wild blue yonder. You can almost see Indian braves off in the distance riding bareback on their paints.

You are once again in the outskirts of the Texas Hill Country. It's not as luxuriant as Kerrville, but after the jaunt into the desert it seems lush. A sign warns that the next two miles are a cattle crossing. Watch for strays.

This hilly, solitary ride features long, rolling, ribbon hills. Watch for water on the road and also road kill. Don't battle with the vultures; let them eat their fill. There are some not-too-difficult curves. The Turkey Mountains rise around you, and make you want to pay more attention to the scenic beauty than to your riding. Beware of a low water crossing over the West Prong of the Nueces River. You'll come over a hill and around a steep curve. All of a sudden the road may be under water. The sign says 35 mph; believe it. You don't want your bike to go swimming. If you want to get wet, park your bike by the side of the river and take a dip.

Turn right at TX 55. The paving is better than on FM 334, and there are still lots of curves to enjoy. You'll cross the Nueces River at a picturesque spot with small rapids, a good place for a rest stop. As you enter Uvalde, turn right to go into town. The well-kept lawns imply a pleasant community. A local store advertises both liquor and guns and has a sign that says, "Welcome Hunters."

Uvalde to Hondo

When you reach US 90 again, turn east (left) towards Uvalde and Hondo. If you want to stop to see the sights you passed on the way out, this is your second chance.

Hondo to Castroville

Continue on US 90 to Hondo. Exit right off US 90 to go left on TX 173. Go about 1.5 miles to FM 2676 and turn right. Now is the time to get off the straight and narrow and have some excitement. The road starts off with a few good curves and gently sloping hills through farmland. Then the hills get hillier and the curves get curvier. For the 18 miles to Riomedina you will experience corkscrew turns with great mountain views in the distance.

Riomedina comes into view in the distance but then disappears and reappears as you travel on. Take a right at FM 471. Castroville is six miles down the road. The detour adds about ten extra miles to the ride, compared to going straight on US 90. But these ten miles are well worth it. You will know you are coming into Castroville when you see some stone houses.

Highlights Along the Way

Castroville. Founded by Henri Castro and settled by Alsatian immigrants. Many original buildings on the walking tour of the town are marked with plaques. www.castroville.com.

Das Haus aus Elsass. Built in the early 1600s in France, the house was disassembled and rebuilt here. Furnished in authentic Alsatian style. 830/538-3142, www.castroville.com.

Landmark Inn State Historic Site. Originally a stagecoach stop, the inn was restored to 1940s era. Interpretive center, water-powered gristmill, and a few rooms for rent. Visible from US 90, 402 E. Florence St. 830/931-2133, www.tpwd.state.us/park.

Hondo. www.hondotex.com.

Graff's Real Estate, Cattle Company, & Antiques. Sells it all. 1116 18th St. 830/741-5845.

Medina County Museum. Nineteenth century train depot filled with pioneer artifacts and exhibits from the area. 2202 18th St. www.epodunk.com.

South Texas Maze. A giant maze in a cornfield. US 90 west of Hondo 830/741-3968, www.cornfieldmaze.com.

777 Exotic Game Ranch. 15,000-acre ranch with exotic animals, movie set for "Ace Ventura—When Nature Calls" and others. Safari-style hunts. Left on Richter Lane, two miles west of Hondo off US 90. Follow the signs to ranch headquarters. 830/426-3476, www.777ranch.com.

D'Hanis.
J. M. Koch Hotel. Restored to a B & B with 5 large bedrooms and 3 large porches. Faces US 90 but on the other side of the tracks. 877/248-4096, www.bbonline.com/tx/jmkoch.

Uvalde.
Garner Memorial Museum and Vice Presidential Library. Former home of John "Cactus Jack" Garner, vice president under F. D. R. Historical displays of the era. 333 N. Park St. 830/278-5018, www.texas-on-line.com/graphic/Uvalde.htm.

Garner State Park: Tubing, swimming, miniature gold, hiking, camping, C & W dancing summer nights. 31 miles north of Uvalde at the junction of US 84 and FM 1050. 830/232-6132, www.tpwd.state.tx.us/park.

Brackettville.
Fort Clark Springs. On the site of Fort Clark, established in 1852. Barracks converted to motel, also restaurant, RV park, and spring-fed swimming pool, Old Guardhouse Museum. On US 90. 210/563-2493, www.fortclark.com.

Alamo Village. Movie set for John Wayne's 1959 Alamo film. Recreation of the Alamo, a frontier town, and more. Entertainment in the summer. On RM 674, 7 miles north of US 90. 830/563-2580, www.alamovillage.com.

Del Rio. Information on the Del Rio area is included in the following description of the Ride across Time.

Ride 18: A Ride Across Time
Del Rio to Fort Stockton

Few expanses of Texas road record human habitation from prehistory to today. As you vroooom along a smooth four-lane divided highway on your high-tech bike with a cell phone and GPS, stopping to use a digital camera and take a swig of bottled water, you'll gaze across the same landscapes as the prehistoric peoples who created the well-preserved pictographs in local caves.

According to archeological research, this area had been inhabited by Indian groups for 10,000 years before Europeans arrived on the scene. Graphic evidence of these ancient inhabitants has been discovered in some 400 archaeological sites throughout the region, making this among the richest areas for aboriginal cave painting in the entire United States. Some, like those in the Amistad National Recreation Area, are accessible only by boat or by foot. Strenuous guided hiking tours lead visitors down to 4,000-year-old rock art in Seminole Canyon State Park. Whether you trek to see the actual paintings, view reproductions in a museum, or merely ride on through, there is something about knowing that ancients traveled this same path that forges a bond with the past.

In between the two time periods represented by the pictographs and your high tech bike is the Wild West world of Judge Roy Bean and the days of westward expansion. This Ride across Time also goes through Langtry, Texas, the home of the colorful Judge Roy Bean, the "Law West of the Pecos," who administered his own brand of frontier justice.

This ride can be a continuation of the Road to Mexico ride (Ride 17). Instead of circling back to Castroville, continue on from Del Rio. Then, when you reach Fort Stockton, you can either proceed on to the Wild West Adventure Rides or rocket on back to San Antonio on I-10.

Getting Started: Del Rio to Sanderson

Del Rio calls itself "The Best of the Border," and for good reason. For a bit of Mexican flavor before embarking on this ride, zip across the border to Ciudad Acuña to enjoy some tasty vittles, nightlife, or old-fashioned shopping. You can leave your bike on the US side of the border and take local transportation.

But if you're anxious to hit the road, head west on US 90. This thoughtful town has timed its lights, so you can usually zip on through without stopping. Even though Del Rio is about three miles long, it doesn't seem that if you go with the flow and maintain the legal speed.

Friendly folks at the Visitors Center just outside of town are full of good information they are happy to share with you. They will tell you that the farther west you go, the more expensive fuel gets. So be sure to top off your tank before too long. You might just save a few pennies down the way. Also make sure you have any other provisions you might need, as there aren't many places to stop for food or other necessities once you leave the Del Rio area. Although there is a small "town" about every twenty to twenty-five miles, the distance a stage coach could trav-

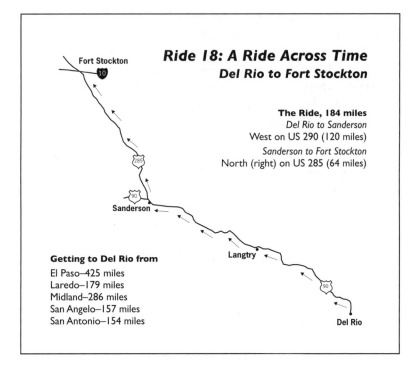

Ride 18: A Ride Across Time
Del Rio to Fort Stockton

Fort Stockton

The Ride, 184 miles
Del Rio to Sanderson
West on US 290 (120 miles)
Sanderson to Fort Stockton
North (right) on US 285 (64 miles)

Sanderson

Getting to Del Rio from
El Paso–425 miles
Laredo–179 miles
Midland–286 miles
San Angelo–157 miles
San Antonio–154 miles

Langtry

Del Rio

el in a day, many of these towns are too small to provide the services and high grade fuel you might want or need.

The four lanes of divided highway leaving Del Rio go through some great hunting areas. White-tailed deer, wild turkey, javelina, dove, and quail are abundant here. With all this food for the taking, the indigenous people could spend time here, even with the rough, arid terrain. Some of the prey may even find their way to the highway, according to all the deer crossing signs and road kill scattered about.

About twelve miles outside of Del Rio is the dam marking the border between Mexico and Texas and that also creates the Amistad International Reservoir. Amistad means friendship, an appropriate name for the border between two friendly nations. The dam also supports power generation, flood control, and water storage. Follow the dam road to the other side and you are in another country. A sign announces that firearms cannot be carried into Mexico. If you have one, do not cross.

The Amistad National Recreation Area is created from the Pecos, Devils, and Rio Grande rivers. All kinds of water sports, camping, picnicking, and educational programs are available at various sites along more than 850 miles of shoreline. This area abounds with aboriginal cave paintings; unfortunately they are accessible only by boat.

For motorcycles the terrain is, as one biker said, "Pretty decent right here!" With long, low rolling hills, curves and a gradual increase in elevation, the riding is the stuff dreams are made of. You can get on some speed and run the limit. The views of tall, flat mesas off in the distance and the scrubby desert vegetation give the whole area a desolate, mysterious atmosphere. Or maybe it feels that way because it is desolate and mysterious.

Cresting a hill almost makes you feel as if you are flying off the face of the earth

The American and Mexican eagles sit on either side of the border at the Amistad Reservoir.

into the pages of a Zane Grey novel. If the scenery looks familiar, it might be from watching too many old John Wayne westerns. These are the foothills of the Davis Mountains. From here on the terrain gets rockier and rougher.

Although there is not much traffic, delays may be caused by Border Patrol and immigration checkpoints. The side of the road is scoured regularly for footprints in case anyone attempts to come into this country at any place other than an official entry.

About forty miles outside of Del Rio is Seminole Canyon State Park. Park Road 67 leads to the Visitors Center and its museum with reproductions of cave paintings found in the area. If you feel adventurous and hearty, take a guided hike to see them. Otherwise, riding the paved roads in the park is an adventure in itself.

Most of the next eighteen miles to Langtry is four lanes over zippy hills and curves. Legend has it that the town was named by Judge Roy Bean, the "Law West of the Pecos," after his idol, the lovely Lillie Langtry. Maybe the colorful judge did name the town. More likely it was named after a civil engineer who worked on railroad construction in this area. Regardless, the judge and his swift, common-sense frontier justice put Langtry on the map. If a stranger happened to die around Langtry, he always just happened to have the exact amount of cash on his corpse

Judge Roy Bean's rustic saloon is preserved at the Visitors Center in Langtry.

to pay the fine for whatever crime he had committed. Needless to say, Judge Bean rarely found the need to consult his one law book.

The Judge Roy Bean Visitors Center features his rustic saloon, courtroom, and billiards hall. He named his home the Opera House in hopes that he could entice Miss Langtry to make an appearance there. Unfortunately, she never made it during his lifetime, arriving some months after his death. The Visitors Center also has some creative holographic exhibits about the history of the town and judge and an extensive cactus garden complete with identifying markers.

At Dead Man's Gulch, near Langtry, the east and west tracks of the Southern Pacific's Sunset Route from New Orleans to San Francisco were joined together with a silver spike in 1883. Other than that, there's not much near Langtry. The next town, Dryden, is forty-one miles west on US 90. The roads cut through rocks and hills. Banked curves through the mountains and desert make this a superior stretch for riding.

The farther west on US 90 you go, the more curves and hills you'll ride. When the person in front of you shushes over the apex of a hill, he/she vanishes from your sight, at least until you catch up and join the descent.

This is an exhilarating ride, without being excessively dangerous. As always, exercise appropriate caution. The road alternates between one and two lanes each way, with wide shoulders. The occasional passing lane comes in handy if there are other vehicles on the road. Some relatively straight stretches are interrupted by fantastically good curves; then a switchback sneaks in when you least expect it.

On the approach to Sanderson, nineteen miles past Dryden, the altitude begins to decline. Tufts of trees and cactus on the tops of the towering mesas in the distance almost look as if Indian scouts are eyeing rebel bikers on a thrill-seeking adventure. No need to circle up to ward off attacks. These stones have been guarding the valleys since the days before the Seminoles.

Sanderson calls itself the Cactus Capital of the World. At Sanderson, turn right on US 285 and head towards Fort Stockton.

Sanderson to Fort Stockton

Before leaving Sanderson, be sure your tank is topped and you have everything you need. There are no services for sixty-four miles. Be prepared.

The next sixty-four miles run along the Texas Pecos Trail. It is an older road with curves and a gentle ascent, which you may feel in your ears. After going up, the road goes down, providing views of some of the best West Texas landscape around. Regular curves and the corkscrew variety with reduced mileage signs go up and down the hills in great roller-coaster fashion. The normal speed limit here is 75 mph, so you can legally let her rip on the straightaway.

You may or may not see another human, but, even if you do, you won't see many. Instead you'll see windmills, oil wells, cattle, and maybe another new age cowboy on a bike, just like you. This is a great long stretch to enjoy your motorcycle and the world. All has to be right with the universe when there is phenomenal riding like this.

The speed limit reduces in ten-mile increments as you approach Fort Stockton until it reaches 55 mph going into the city. After riding through some of the most rugged and beautiful western landscape around, you'll be ready to stop for a spell in the city.

Fort Stockton, with a population of almost 8,000, has all the goods and services you might possibly need. It is a good place to use as a launching pad for the Big Bend Country rides. Or you can hook a right on I-10 and zip on back the 300 miles to San Antonio, or take a left for the 240 miles to El Paso.

Highlights Along the Way

Del Rio. Walking tour of historic downtown area with buildings and homes dating to the 1800s in this Texas Main Street City. Includes the ancient acequia system, irrigation canals, still in use. www.cityofdelrio.com.

Ciudad Acuña. Del Rio's sister city across the Mexican border. http://www.drchamber.com.

Amistad National Recreation Area. Hiking, camping, water sports in border-forming reservoir the US and Mexico. Cave paintings accessible by boat. Multiple access point off US 90. 830/775-7491, www.nps.gov/amis.

Seminole Canyon State Park. Strenuous hiking tours to the natural rock shelters carved into the canyon by the Pecos River to view ancient cave paintings in the Fate Bell Shelter. Tent camping, interpretive museum, guided tours. US 90 West at Comstock. 432/292-4464, www.tpwd.state.tx.us.

Langtry. Established at the junction of railway construction, but made famous by the colorful Judge Roy Bean. US 90 West.

Judge Roy Bean Visitors Center. Features the rustic saloon, courtroom and billiard hall, and the opera house/home of Judge Roy Bean, the "Law West of the Pecos" in the 1880s. Also extensive labeled cactus garden and informative travel center operated by the Texas Department of Transportation. US 90, sixty miles west of Del Rio. http://www.texasoutside.com/roybeanp2.htm.

Fort Stockton. Established as a military outpost in 1859. Adobe and hand-hewn limestone buildings, some restored and others reconstructed. 300 E. 3rd St. 432/336-2400, http://www.tourtexas.com/fortstockton.

Texas Gulf Coast

The Texas Gulf Coast region is a long, thin region that stretches for 624 miles from the Louisiana border to the Rio Grande. The area has the diversity of cities as well as rural farmlands, but you're never far from the Gulf of Mexico.

This proximity to the water makes the riding calm and relaxing in this region. For the most part the land is flat, and the roads are straight. This makes it possible to travel long distances at a time, so these rides are a bit longer than those in other regions of the state. The Texas Gulf Coast is a place ideal for communing with your bike, yourself, and nature. This is a place to let loose and enjoy the pure delight of riding. These rides are perfect for stress relief as well as fun. These are also rides that are great for those who want a nice, easy-going route to hone their skills.

The Texas Gulf Coast rides are through some of the richest, most fertile, and most productive farmland in the country. Below the surface, this region is also among the richest in other natural resources, especially oil and natural gas.

These rides also go by some of the best playgrounds and beaches in the state. The distances are long, but the rewards of arriving are great. The sheer thrill of getting there is the best reason of all for riding the coast.

Ride 19: The Best of Texas Farmlands
A Pastoral Ride through the Coastal Plains

Just a few minutes south of the hustle of sprawling Houston you can experience rural peace. With constant traffic, road construction, and all the hassles of city living, you need to escape it all by riding through some of the prettiest farmland in America. Agriculture is the backbone of Texas and still one of the most important sectors of our economy. When you take this ride, forget the traumas of daily life and just enjoy.

This ride passes sites that commemorate the Lone Star State's illustrious past and its agrarian roots. Cotton, rice, sorghum, soybeans, grass, and hay are a few of the crops growing in the fields along this bucolic route. But even when the crops have been harvested and plowed under, the row after row of rich black soil mounded into straight rows is a sight to behold. In between fields of cropland are acres and acres of pasture land. This is the real Texas, a land of hard-working, down-to-earth, independent, flag-waving folks.

The Best of Texas Farmlands ride follows parts of the Greater Texas Birding Trail that more than 200 species of migratory birds travel as they fly north from Mexico in the summer and then points south to their winter homes. Keep in mind that if you get splat, especially in the early spring, it might be from an endangered species. That won't make it clean off your windshield or helmet any easier, but it does make for a better story to tell.

For the most part, roads on this ride are smooth, flat, and straight. There is generally little traffic. The most common road hazard will be a slow tractor or a farmer in a pickup checking out his crops and those of his neighbors. The easy roads make this an ideal ride for novices and families. However, there are just enough curves and turns to keep even the most experienced biker happy. Be one with your bike, yourself, and your world as you ride through some of the state's best farmland.

Getting Started: US 59 to Brazos Bend State Park

When you exit US 59 onto FM 762 you have a choice. You can go north to visit the historic section of Richmond, or you can begin this ride by turning south. Unless you are too anxious to hit the road, take a circuit through the old city.

Times have changed in Richmond since the days when Carrie Nation began her crusade against "demon rum" here. Now libations are certainly available, along with almost every other type of goods and services you might need for your bike. There is a lot of history here. The Fort Bend Museum focuses on the original Anglo-American colonists who settled in this part of Spanish Texas and their leader, Stephen F. Austin. A number of historic homes are part of the museum complex, including the Long-Smith Cottage, built on land originally owned by Jane Long, the Mother of Texas. Her land grant included most of what is now the city of Richmond.

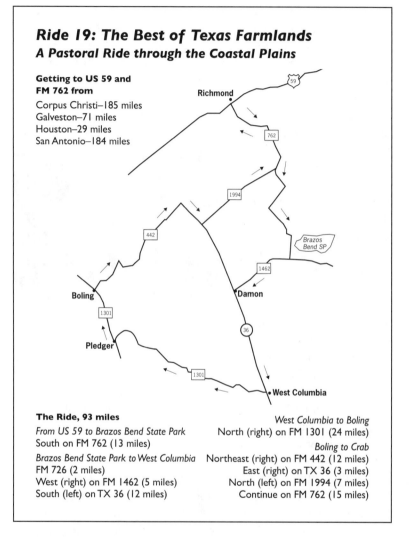

Ride 19: The Best of Texas Farmlands
A Pastoral Ride through the Coastal Plains

**Getting to US 59 and
FM 762 from**

Corpus Christi–185 miles
Galveston–71 miles
Houston–29 miles
San Antonio–184 miles

Richmond

59

762

1994

442

Brazos
Bend SP

1462

Boling

1301

Damon

36

Pledger

1301

• West Columbia

The Ride, 93 miles

From US 59 to Brazos Bend State Park
South on FM 762 (13 miles)

Brazos Bend State Park to West Columbia
FM 726 (2 miles)
West (right) on FM 1462 (5 miles)
South (left) on TX 36 (12 miles)

West Columbia to Boling
North (right) on FM 1301 (24 miles)

Boling to Crab
Northeast (right) on FM 442 (12 miles)
East (right) on TX 36 (3 miles)
North (left) on FM 1994 (7 miles)
Continue on FM 762 (15 miles)

When you are ready to start riding, turn south on FM 762. The speed limit starts at 55 mph. The two-lane road has a few curves, and there are deep ditches off both sides. At the stop sign, turn right, following the sign to stay on FM 762 towards George Ranch and Brazos Bend State Park. Cross the railroad tracks and you are in the country. Crops and pastures are off to the side. Unfortunately, there is evidence that Houston sprawl is starting to creep in.

For the most part, the terrain on this ride will be smooth, flat, and straight. However, every rule has its exceptions, and the first one is just a couple of miles into the ride. A sharp curve to the left sneaks up on you, so be careful. Some farmhouses dot the side of the road. Occasionally one is much larger than the others. Cotton fields stretch as far as the eye can see.

The entrance to the George Ranch Historical Park is in about four miles. You'll know to watch for it after you have passed two good curves, both with reduced mileage signs, and then see longhorn cattle grazing off to your right. The park has three distinct historical habitats: a farmstead of the 1820s, an 1890s Victorian mansion, and a working ranch from the 1930s. Each section has hands-on experiences, and gives a good view of different times in Texas history.

Beware of dangerous inhabitants lurking at Brazos Bend State Park.

Come back to FM 762 after your stop, or, if you choose not to linger here, continue on. FM 762 is a straight, smooth, blacktop road at this point, but there are still a few good curves with reduced mileage signs. The country here is pretty in its own way, flat and fertile.

About seven miles after leaving George Ranch Historical Park, FM 762 makes a sharp turn to the left at the blinker at the junction with FM 1994. Make the turn, and stay on FM 762.

With all of the great straightaways, it's easy to get in the zone and coast along at good speeds. But there are just enough curves here to mandate that you stay alert in spite of the smooth riding. You don't want to end up in one of the deep ditches on the side of the road.

Turn left into Brazos Bend State Park. Lots of signs won't let you miss the turn. Park Road 72 takes you into the park with fun curves and twists. Read the warnings on the official map you will be handed as you enter the park: "Don't feed the alligators," "Snakes may be poisonous," and "Plants and wildlife are protected by law." All the warnings might make you want to turn around, but it is still a good place to visit; just be sure to stay on the roadways. You might want to come back on a

Saturday evening when the George Observatory with its three domed telescopes is open to the public. The Nature Center is open daily.

Brazos Bend State Park to West Columbia

Continue down FM 762 another two miles beyond the cutoff to the park. The road dead-ends into FM 1462 at Woodrow. Two gas stations are located at the intersection. Turn west (right) and ride about five miles to the junction with TX 36 at Damon. Head southwest (left) towards West Columbia. Damon is a farm town with a cotton gin, a couple of watering holes, and lots of churches. At one time a patent medicine named Vitae Orr was made from the sour dirt around here. The biggest traffic hazard will be slow tractors and turning pickups.

TX 36 is a state highway with wide shoulders and steep drop-offs, lots of trees, and only a few houses along the side. Rice, cotton, other crops, and pasture land extend as far as the horizon. This is a great stretch to let loose and go.

A few houses mark the approach to West Columbia. The first duly elected Congress of the Republic of Texas met in 1836 in Columbia, as the town was called back then, under a triple-trunk live oak tree known as the Independence Tree. So many people moved to the area while it was the capital that the congress voted to move to Houston the next year. Artifacts and exhibits about the early days of Texas and the role this area played are in the Columbia Historical Museum.

During the war with Mexico, Santa Anna camped out at what is now Varner Hogg State Park. To detour to the park, follow the signs and turn left on FM 1301, also called Brazos Street. This will take you through a commercial area of a few stores and churches. Turn left at the light and follow the signs through a modest residential area to the park. The road ends at the entrance of the park and Park Road 51. Moss dripping from the trees seems to lower the temperature by at least ten degrees as soon as you enter the gates. Watch for snakes.

Carrie Nation once ran a hotel in Columbia. Maybe that is why she began her temperance tour in nearby Richmond.

West Columbia to Boling

Retrace your steps to FM 1301. Go straight across TX 36. Or, if you choose not to visit the park, turn right at the intersection of TX 36 and FM 1301 on your way into town. After a couple of mild curves you'll be in the open country again. The terrain is mostly flat and straight through fertile farmland. This is America's country. People living along this road proudly display their patriotism by flying the American flag in front of their property.

Ride the gentle curves, but watch the loose gravel or grass that borders the roadway instead of shoulders. Critters live in the grasslands and woods all around. They come out and unsuspecting motorists hit them. Watch out for road kill as well as for the living wildlife itself.

Although this ride is mostly straight, just when you think the road will never turn again another curve with a slow mileage sign pops up. There are lots of nice pastures, scattered trees, idyllic views, and cattle lounging around under the few trees. You will probably even see a few other bikes. The bikers you meet on this stretch will almost certainly be loners, too, or maybe a pair at most.

Just before reaching the Wharton County line, FM 1301 makes a sharp turn north (right). Down the road a bit is a picturesque ranch with a wide, curving stream flowing in front. Some of the trees are surprisingly tall for this area.

At the junction with FM 442 in Boling, turn northeast (right) at the blinking red light and stop sign. There is a gas station here for fuel and beverages if you or your tank is running on empty. Boling was a boomtown beginning in the mid 1920s when sulfur, oil, and gas were discovered here. Unfortunately, the boom did not last. Leaving Boling, you pass some fancy homes and orchards of pecan trees.

Boling Back to the Beginning

On FM 442 you'll pass Acorn Acres, a nudist resort. Biker groups have been known to plan events here. You'll have to research that yourself.

Turn right at the intersection with TX 36. Although the sign points the way to West Columbia, you will turn north (left) at FM 1994 in a couple of miles. At the blinker about seven miles on, you'll realize you are on FM 762, the very same road you started on.

Highlights Along the Way

Richmond. Historic city. www.richmond.tx.net.

Fort Bend Museum: Focuses on Anglo-American settlers, Spanish Texas, and the local influences on the Texas Revolution, Civil War, and agriculture. 500 Houston St. 281-342-1256, www.fortbendmuseum.org.

Long-Smith Cottage. Built in the 1840s on land originally owned by Jane Long, Mother of Texas. Tour of the cottage is available through the Fort Bend Museum.

George Ranch Historical Park. A living history museum where visitors can experience the 1820s Jones farmstead, tour a 1890s Victorian mansion, and see cowboys working cattle as they did in the 1930s. 10215 FM 762, eight miles south of Rosenberg. 281/545-9212, www.georgeranch.org.

Brazos Bend State Park. Nearly 5,000 acres of Gulf Coast prairies with diverse ecologies, including lakes and bayous complete with alligators and other wildlife. Hiking trails, picnicking, and camping. 21901 FM 762, Needville. 979/553-5101, www.tpwd.state.tx.us/park/brazos.

George Observatory: Located in the park. Features three domed telescopes, the largest a 36-inch Gueymard Research Telescope. Open for viewing on Saturday evenings. 713/639-4629, www.hmns.org.

West Columbia.

Columbia Historical Museum. The museum concentrates on the role of this area in Texas history, including the Texas Revolution, formation of the Republic of Texas, oil industry, and agriculture. 247 E. Brazos St. (TX 35). 979/345-6125, www.westcolumbia.org.

Varner Hogg State Park. Formerly a sugar plantation owned by the first native-born Texan governor, the park features a restored antebellum mansion. Picnicking, nature trails, day use only. 1702 N. 17th St. 979/345-4656, www.tpwd.state.tx.us/park/varner.

Ride 20: High Energy
West Columbia to Port Lavaca

This ride along the Texas Gulf Coast may look pastoral and serene, with waves lapping onto the shore, fishermen baiting their hooks, and cattle grazing in fields. But under the surface, this region of Texas brims with energy.

Much of the energy and power produced in Texas comes from around here. On this ride you'll see rigs and pumps producing the black gold called oil that Texas is so famous for. It might not be as easy to get to as it once was, but the oil industry still pumps away. Together with the oil is natural gas that sometimes still burns in flares. You won't see much of that on this ride. The newbie on the energy scene is nuclear power. This ride also passes the nuclear power plant in Matagorda. But you'll have to admire it from afar, because post-9/11 security won't let you in close.

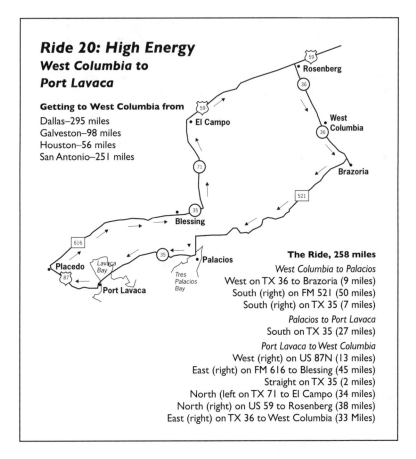

Ride 20: High Energy
West Columbia to
Port Lavaca

Getting to West Columbia from
Dallas–295 miles
Galveston–98 miles
Houston–56 miles
San Antonio–251 miles

The Ride, 258 miles

West Columbia to Palacios
West on TX 36 to Brazoria (9 miles)
South (right) on FM 521 (50 miles)
South (right) on TX 35 (7 miles)

Palacios to Port Lavaca
South on TX 35 (27 miles)

Port Lavaca to West Columbia
West (right) on US 87N (13 miles)
East (right) on FM 616 to Blessing (45 miles)
Straight on TX 35 (2 miles)
North (left on TX 71 to El Campo (34 miles)
North (right) on US 59 to Rosenberg (38 miles)
East (right) on TX 36 to West Columbia (33 Miles)

These signs of our industrial civilization are tucked into corners of some of the richest and most beautiful farmland and pasture land in the country. When settlers first came, they did not have to go far inland to make their fortunes. Everything they needed was right here: access to the gulf for shipping, trade, and fishing, and a place to grow crops. As a hub for communications, unrest with Mexico flourished here in the early 1800s. This was a hot spot in the quest for Texas Independence.

One of the best features of this ride is that it can be an extension of the Best of Texas Farmlands ride (Ride 19). This ride can also be continued into the Past and Present Texas ride (Ride 21) that goes from Victoria to Corpus Christi, depending on how much time you have and how far you want to go. For those diehard iron butts with steel constitutions this ride can extend into the Valley Ride (Ride 23). Link them together or do one or two at a time. Whichever way you choose, you're in for a fine time.

Getting Started: West Columbia to Palacios

This ride starts when you get on FM 521, one of the great coastal roads in this part of the state. It travels through areas important to Texas—farms, oil fields, and nuclear power, all critical to today's economy and the power sources of tomorrow. One good place to get on FM 521 is between West Columbia and Angleton. If you want to add more miles to the Best of Texas Farmlands ride, head east on TX 36 from West Columbia for about nine miles until you reach FM 521. Take a right and head south towards Brazoria.

Or, to bypass West Columbia altogether, turn left instead of right when you get to the intersection of FM 762 and FM 1462 on the Farmlands ride. Then take a right (south) when you come to FM 521.

However you get there, you'll be glad you did. The road is wide, straight and easy. It's almost hard to believe that all the hustle and bustle of Houston is not many miles away. Here you feel as if you have escaped the city, the rat race, and the pollution. The bridge over the Brazos River as you are coming into town is one of those fortress-looking, old-fashioned steel bridges with buttresses overhead.

Traffic or congestion when you enter Brazoria is of the small town variety, nothing at all like the big cities. Turn left at the light toward Wadsworth where FM 521 W joins TX 36 S. As you cross the tracks, you'll see the railroad mural painted on the side of the Brazoria Hardware store. As you trek through the small towns of Texas, especially those along the coast, you'll see a number of these murals depicting the history of the area on the sides of stores and public buildings. Say something nice about the murals to any townsfolk you meet. They are justifiably proud of their communities.

Brazoria is called the "Cradle of Texas" because so much happened in the Brazoria/Brazosport area. A lot of this history is preserved at the Brazoria County Historical Museum.

Turn right at the light onto FM 521 to go to Wadsworth. The intersection is not well marked, but go ahead and take the right bypass around the light. In no time at all, you'll be riding on some nice, long gentle curves through gorgeous pasture land. The overpass that goes above Oyster Creek may be a man-made hill, but it still provides a nice view of the area.

Spanish moss dripping from trees gives the area a calm, pastoral atmosphere, which is exactly how you'll feel unless you get caught behind a slow tractor. But even if you do, passing should not be a problem here. As easy as it is to get into the groove and coast along, be aware that Cedar Lane has a blinking red light. Stop, look, and go.

Crossing so many creeks and rivers is one of the best features of this ride. One particularly picturesque crossing is over Live Oak Creek about fifteen miles outside of Brazoria. As you approach Wadsworth you will ride around some gentle curves, a few with reduced speeds, and over some minor hills. A switchback and 90-degree corkscrew will spice up the otherwise bucolic ride. At Wadsworth, take a left hand jog on TX 60 and then a right to get back on FM 521.

Birds migrating to or from their summer homes in Mexico and other points south may be flying overhead. This area is part of the Greater Texas Birding Trail. Over two hundred species of birds have been sighted in these parts.

Before you have traveled the seven miles down the two flat, straight lanes to the South Texas Project Electric Generating Station—the South Texas Nuclear Power Plant—you'll spy the huge domes growing out of the prairie. As you come around a curve they magically appear in the distance, a sight almost as surreal as the domes themselves. Don't even think about riding up to the guardhouse; you will be turned away. To find out what's going on there, stop across the street at the Frank T. Harrison, Jr. Visitor Center. That is about as close as you can get.

Huge towers support thick power lines transporting electricity to all corners of this part of the state. The towers and power lines draw straight lines through cotton and rice fields for hundreds of miles.

On the left is South Texas Nuclear Power Plant Lake, no fishing. The blinking light at the intersection with FM 1095 points the way to College Port, a remnant of a once thriving college town that faced too many hurricanes to survive. A few miles farther down is Simpsonville, known to the locals as Tin Top, after the establishment at the intersection.

Take a left at the junction with TX 35 at the blinker and head towards Palacios, population 5,153. Follow Business TX 35 into town and cruise down to Bayshore Drive. Stretch your legs on the paved seaside walk, breathe the fresh salt air and enjoy the picnic tables, palm trees, and playgrounds. Or spend the night at the historic Luther Hotel, built in 1903. During its glory days, a tuxedo-clad orchestra played at meal-times for land developers who stayed there. This is one of the few old

wooden hotels in Texas still regularly receiving guests.

This port is home to the largest fishing fleet on the Texas Gulf coast. If you get an irresistible urge to eat shrimp or catfish, stop in at the Outrigger

A gazebo is the focal point of this quiet park in Palacios, home port of the largest fishing fleet on the Texas Gulf coast.

Restaurant or any other seafood places. Relax at the picturesque gazebo across the street from the Outrigger. A free fishing pier with a covered pavilion stretches into the Tres Palacios Bay. The bay got its name from some shipwrecked Spaniards who supposedly saw a vision of tres palacios—three palaces—as they swam ashore.

Palacios to Port Lavaca

When you are ready to continue, take Main Street out of town past a big curve and then past the airport. After riding through a few miles of cotton fields and pastures, you'll see a lot of beach houses on stilts towering above the water. This protects them from flooding when a hurricane blows through. On the left is Carancahua Bay, named after the native cannibals who lived here when the first explorers arrived.

A picnic area is situated in the shade of the Alcoa Plant at Point Comfort. Here you will see a sign to Lolita. Don't turn off yet; this ride will take you there later.

On TX 35 near the Port Lavaca Causeway is the Halfmoon Reef Lighthouse. During the War Between the States the lighthouse was kept dark to aid blockade-runners. It was reactivated after the Civil

War, lighting the way until it was damaged by a hurricane in 1942. After several moves, it ended up here.

The causeway over the Lavaca Bay is more than two miles of four-lane highway. Once you cross it and get into Port Lavaca, you'll see signs to the interesting and historic sights in this area. The Lighthouse Beach and Bird Sanctuary has a beautiful sandy beach, waterfront camping sites, a swimming pool, and the Alcoa Bird Tower, made completely out of recycled plastic, for bird watching.

An interesting side trip from Port Lavaca is south on TX 316 to the Indianola County Historical Park. La Salle is thought to have first landed in Texas in 1685 at Indianola. In the 1800s it was considered the best seaport on the Gulf of Mexico; its piers jutted half a mile into the bay. At one point, two boatloads of camels where brought in to transport cargo at the port. All the prosperity came to an end when two hurricanes, a decade apart, leveled the city. Today there is little more than the remains of a once-thriving city, a stature commemorating La Salle, and the ghosts of the thousands who perished.

Leave Port Lavaca on US 87 N as if going to Victoria. The road starts out as a typical four lane US highway, but soon narrows to two lanes. But that's okay because there is so little traffic on the straightaway. At this point, if you want to add on the Victoria to Corpus Christi ride, take US 87 North to US 59 just outside of Victoria and go to Past and Present Texas (Ride 21) to follow that ride. If you're ready to head back to where you began, turn right onto FM 616 at Placeda.

This is real country riding. Just you and the jackrabbits share the long stretches of rural road. If it weren't for the railroad tracks, the electric lines, and a very few houses, you might think you were the first one to ride in these parts. The landscape is largely pasture and coastal marshland. You'll ride through the communities of La Salle and Vanderbilt. At Lolita turn left at the dead end and then right just after the railroad tracks to stay on FM 616.

Keep going straight through La Ward, and don't blink when you go through Francitas. This is hunting country, so, especially during deer season, stay on the roads and out of the private land behind the fences. You don't want to be mistaken for a buck or a doe. The terrain becomes a bit more interesting as you tool along, with more baby hills and trees. Be sure to watch out for road kill in your path.

Danish and American flags fly at the Danish Heritage Museum in Danevang.

If you get to Blessing at lunchtime, be sure to stop at the Blessing Hotel for the all-you-can-eat buffet. Built in the early 1900s to lure land investors to the area, this hotel and the Luther Hotel in Palacios are the only two wooden hotels standing in Coastal Texas that still shelter guests. Its modern-day fame is due to the home cooked buffet served in the dining room.

Continue straight on FM 616, which becomes TX 35 out of Blessing. An interesting side trip is to the Hawley cemetery, which dates back to 1854. It's a peaceful, well-maintained old graveyard with big trees, some dripping with Spanish moss. One of the more colorful residents of this cemetery is A.H. Pierce, also known as Shanghai Pierce. After a night of debauchery in Palacios, he woke up the next day on a ship headed for Shanghai, China, a popular way of getting hands to crew ships back in the eighteen hundreds. Shanghai managed to get back to his native Texas, where he continued to live a colorful life. The Pierce family was a wealthy and powerful force back in those days. There is even a small town named after them.

If you take this detour, backtrack on TX 35 to the intersection with TX 71 and go north. This is another smooth, straight road through fields and pastures that passes a herd of longhorns.

The next interesting place to take a break is the community of Danevang, declared "The Danish Capital of Texas" by the state legislature. You'll know you are there when you see a large, barn-like structure with the red and white Danish flag painted on the side off to your right.

The Danevang Cultural Center consists of an 1896 Pioneer House; the Hansen Shed, a farm museum; and the Danish Cultural Museum. Stop in for some interesting exhibits on the Vikings and local nostalgia. Cold drinks are in the fridge in the kitchen. You're on your honor to drop the right amount of change into the bowl on the second shelf above the drinks.

About nine miles north on TX 71 is the junction with US 59, just outside El Campo. Turn right and head towards Houston. This is fast US highway riding that bypasses most of the lights and blinkers of towns along the way.

If you get hungry, Hinze's Bar BQ on the far side of Wharton serves some tasty Que you might want to try. Dan Rather is a native of Wharton, also Horton Foote, author of the screenplay for Harper Lee's novel *To Kill a Mockingbird*. Rather's childhood home is on the grounds of the Wharton Country Historical Museum. Otherwise scoot back up US 59. Cut off to go back to West Columbia, unless you're headed somewhere else down the road.

Highlights Along the Way

Palacios. www.palaciostexas.com.
Luther Hotel. A Texas Historic Landmark, now a B & B. 4095 Bayshore Dr., between 4th and 5th Streets. 361/972-2312.
Outrigger Restaurant. Seafood, steaks and barbeque. 515 Commerce St. 361/972-1499, www.outriggerrestaurant.com.

Port Lavaca. www.portlavaca.com.
Lighthouse Beach and Bird Sanctuary. Beach, camping, swimming pool, playgrounds, birding. Also, the Formosa Wetlands Walkway and Alcoa Bird Tower. www.portlavaca.org/tosee/sights.htm.

Blessing Hotel. One of the few old wooden hotels still standing in Texas. Huge buffet breakfast, lunch. Blessing. 361/588-6623, www.hotelblessing.com.

Danish Cultural Center: Museum complex dedicated to the local Danish culture and Viking heritage. Danevang. US 71 and CR 426. 979/543-3332, http://dkhouston.org/danim/DHPSD.pdf.

Wharton.
Wharton County Historical Museum: Wildlife trophies, and artifacts relating to Wharton County history, including agriculture, medicine, and local sulfur mines. Home of Dan Rather on the grounds. 3615 N. Richmond Rd. 979/532-2600, www.newgulftexas.com/museum.
Hinze Bar-B-Q: Bar-B-Q, trimmings. 3940 US 59. 979/532-2710.

Ride 21: Past and Present Texas
Port Lavaca to Corpus Christi

This route begins where the High Energy ride turns around to go back to the beginning. If you continue, you will ride through more of the beautiful Texas Gulf Coast along TX 35, considered by many bikers to be one of the best roads in this part of the state. When you reach Corpus Christi, the end of this ride, you may be tempted to continue on the Sun, Surf, and Sea Ride to South Padre Island for even more great coastal riding.

On the other hand, these extensions can be saved for another day. Once you reach the apex of this route, turn back to the north and enjoy an excursion into the South Texas Plains. The road morphs from flat, straight runways to gentle hills and curves. The terrain changes from marshes and low-lying farmlands to lush green forests and pastures. Underground wonders, ranging from relics of peoples past to oil and uranium for our present and future, are found along this route.

The entire area covered in this ride is rich in history. From the seaports that brought in immigrants and shipped goods out to the early missions and battlegrounds of the Texas Revolution, everywhere you look some event of significance occurred. With shipping, commerce, agriculture, and energy, this is also an area extremely important to the present as well as the future of our state and nation.

But even more important to right now is the riding. Here you will experience long stretches of tender riding, with enough variations to keep you fascinated. Yet the riding here is mild enough to let your brain and soul release any clutter. When you eventually park your bike at the end of the ride you will feel as if you have been transported to another world and returned to a better one.

Getting started: Victoria to Port Lavaca

A good place to start this trek is at the Skillet Restaurant at the intersection of US 87 and US 59, just southeast of Victoria. Have a hearty breakfast, regardless of the time of day, before beginning this 225-mile ride.

The four lane divided highway, which narrows to two lanes after a few miles, is smooth and straight, for the most part. Although the surrounding rice, cotton, and pasture land is flat and mainly straight, over-

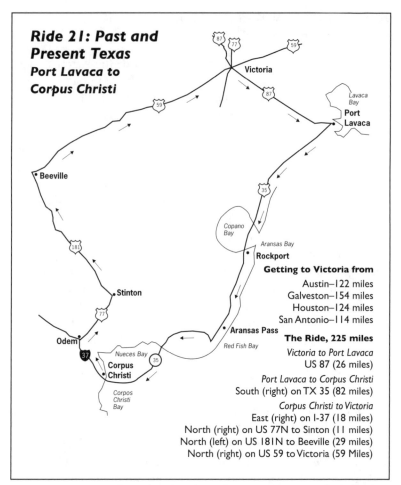

Ride 21: Past and Present Texas
Port Lavaca to
Corpus Christi

Victoria

Lavaca
Bay

Port
Lavaca

Beeville

Copano
Bay

Aransas Bay

Rockport

Getting to Victoria from
Austin–122 miles
Galveston–154 miles
Houston–124 miles
San Antonio–114 miles

Stinton

Aransas Pass
Red Fish Bay

The Ride, 225 miles

Victoria to Port Lavaca
US 87 (26 miles)

Port Lavaca to Corpus Christi
South (right) on TX 35 (82 miles)

Odem

Nueces Bay

Corpus
Christi

Corpus Christi to Victoria
East (right) on I-37 (18 miles)
North (right) on US 77N to Sinton (11 miles)
North (left) on US 181N to Beeville (29 miles)
North (right) on US 59 to Victoria (59 Miles)

Corpos
Christi
Bay

passes crossing roads and railroad tracks create man-made hills that provide some nice views of the surrounding areas. Sprouting throughout the countryside are Christmas trees—not the holiday pine variety, but, rather, the oil pumping kind. This easy, relaxing riding is perfect for communing with your bike and nature. Here you can get into the groove and go.

Although there are a number of driveways off the main road, there is very little cross traffic. Fortunately, US 87 intersects TX 35 outside of Port Lavaca, so you can miss any traffic there. Go southwest (right) towards Corpus Christi on TX 35.

At FM 2433, you'll see the sign pointing the way to Indianola, probably the biggest, most successful city in Texas to become a ghost town. Once a thriving seaport considered the best on the Gulf Coast, Indianola was flattened twice by hurricanes only a decade apart. Now it is a watery reminder of nature's power.

Port Lavaca to Corpus Christi

TX 35 follows the Texas Gulf Coast all the way to Corpus Christi and beyond. From here there are many bridges crossing rivers and bays along the coast. The road goes through and by some of the more interesting ecological areas in the state, many are preserved in wildlife refuges or management areas. These are good places to stop, relax, sightsee, or zoom on by, your choice.

Much of this route is on the Greater Texas Birding Trail. More than 200 varieties of birds pass over this area on their way to their winter homes in Mexico and points farther south. They fly over again on their way back to their summer homes in the northern areas of the US and Canada. The road passes over the Victoria Barge Canal, part of the Intracoastal Waterway, and by the Guadalupe Wildlife Management Area.

Austwell, on the way to the Aransas Wildlife Refuge on TX 239, is one place that endangered whooping cranes may be sighted. One of the best ways to view wildlife at the refuge, especially the whoopers, is by boat.

The way to Rockport is smooth and straight through coastal flatlands. Holiday Beach, just before the bridge to Rockport, is, as the name suggests, a place to go for the joy of the beach. You will probably run into other bikers out for the fun and beauty of riding along the many bays and Gulf of Mexico. Fishing and RVing are other ubiquitous activities around here. One of the big hazards is getting stuck behind a slow pick-up truck towing a big fishing boat. Before you lose patience, keep in mind that, since the water is so close and boat ramps are almost everywhere, it will be turning off before long.

Goose Island State Park is another good place to stop for a break. Here you might spot brown pelicans or even one of the few nearly extinct whooping cranes. This island is also the home of the "Big Tree," an immense oak estimated to be a thousand years old and certified as the

Stop to birdwatch in Port Lavaca at the Lighthouse Beach and Bird Sanctuary's Alcoa Bird Tower, made entirely out of recycled plastic.

largest in the state. There are restrooms, showers, picnic sites, camping, and a swimming beach.

The bridge over the bay to Rockport is about two miles of riding fun. Because Rockport is a port, large ships have to pass under the bridge. That makes the bridge one of the highest and best hills in the area, with an added element of excitement—any altercation with traffic can result in a serious need to swim. On the right side of the bridge is the Copano Bay State Fishing Pier, formerly a bridge. The east side of the bridge looks over Aransas Bay.

Skirt around Rockport on TX 35 S by taking a right to avoid the business route through town. After about eleven miles of smooth riding you'll see the cutoff to Port Aransas on Mustang Island, another good place for birding, fishing, and other beach activities. Mustang Island State Park has five miles of Gulf beach frontage that offer some of the best seaside camping anywhere.

All along TX 35 you'll pass cotton fields and refineries, two of the most important contributors to the Texas economy that produce two of the main cargoes passing through the port of Corpus Christi. To continue riding and avoid most of the city traffic in Corpus Christi, take the US 181/77 cut-off towards Sinton and Gregory. Those who choose to go into Corpus Christi will catch up with you later, probably much later because there is so much to see and do here.

To see the sights in Corpus Christi, continue on US 181/TX35 over the seven-mile bridge that arches 235 feet above the water. Looking down, you can see ships from almost every country entering and leaving. Corpus Christi is the fifth largest deep-water port in the United States. Major cargoes are oil and petroleum products, grain, cotton, and chemicals.

There is so much more to the area than just the ship channel. You could easily spend several days touring the USS Lexington, a WWII aircraft carrier that served longer and set more records than any other carrier; the Selena Museum dedicated to the memory of the Tejano singer; the Texas State Aquarium; and many other great places. Good signs point the way to the major sights as you come off the bridge.

Or you can head on down to Ocean Drive, a seven-mile scenic stretch along the waterfront. Between Ocean Drive and the gulf are the downtown seawall and Cole Park, a great place to stop to people watch or to take a dip. Steps lead from the seawall directly down to the beach.

Corpus Christi to Victoria

When you come off the bridge, take I-37 to the west as if you are going to San Antonio. This way misses most of the traffic by zipping around the city. Instead, you'll go past miles and miles of Citgo refineries and oil storage tanks and the Corpus Christi Greyhound Race Track, featuring pari-mutuel wagering.

Since this is an interstate highway, there is a real potential for heavy traffic. If you avoid rush hour you will probably be surprised at how easy the riding is. You'll pass the turn to Padre Island; that will be on another ride.

Leaving Corpus Christi is a good time to check your fuel. There will be places to stop ahead, but why take a chance that they won't have exactly what you need?

Stay on I-37 about eighteen miles after the end of the bridge. Then take a right onto US 77 N toward Odem and Sinton. Don't take US 77 S, which exits first. The road to Odem is four lanes, divided with a nice, wide shoulder. Long, low hills pass through pasture land and crops. Odem has three stoplights and a railroad crossing, quite a bit for a town of just 2,500 people. The last weekend of the month is Odem Market Days, a flea market extravaganza.

The next seven miles are easy riding, with smooth, wide curves. Take the US 181 loop just before Sinton and head north (left) toward Beeville. One interesting site you'll pass is Papalote, a town that in its heyday had quite a rollicking reputation. This was where the action was, especially on Saturday night. Stop at a picturesque roadside park and get the lowdown from the historical marker about all the fun you missed.

There are some curves after Papalote on the way to Skidmore. The town has a lowered speed limit, two blinking yellow lights, some gas stations, a Dairy Queen, and a couple of other places. After Skidmore the road gets hillier. There are more curves, because you're going inland and getting out of the coastal prairies and marshlands

Stay on US 181 N until you see the sign to US 59 to George West and Goliad. The road becomes two lanes with a shoulder, a lot like country riding on a US highway, the best of both worlds. The hills are long and gently sloping going through miles of pasture land. Instead of marshes and crops, cactus grows along the side of the road, and the trees are mainly on the banks of creeks where there is water. There is a lot of good hunting around here, so be sure to heed the no-trespassing signs posted everywhere.

This second part of the ride runs through the South Texas Plains region, rather than through the Gulf Coast region of the beginning of the trip. The terrain is different and the sights are different. After Beeville the ride goes through the San Antonio River Valley Historic District. This area overflows with Texas history from the earliest settlements through the Texas Revolution.

Goliad is one of Texas's oldest municipalities, but archeological evidence indicates human habitation here even before recorded history. Historical sites include Goliad State Park, which has a reconstruction of the Mission Espiritu Santo, established by Spaniards in 1749 to Christianize the natives of the area. Two miles south of the city is the Presidio La Bahia, the only fully-restored Spanish presidio in the western hemisphere. Here General Santa Anna ordered the execution of Col. James Fannin and 341 other men, giving rise to the battle cry, "Remember Goliad." A monument marks the graves of these Texas heroes.

Nearby is the Fannin Battleground, where Fannin and his men surrendered to the Mexican army after the Battle of Coleto Creek, thinking they had done so on honorable terms and would receive clemency. For Texas history buffs, this is the start of the Texas Independence Trail that goes through the famous locations every seventh grader learns about in social studies.

In addition to the ride through Texas's illustrious past, the cutoff to Kenedy-Crenant City leads to the future and the site of the only uranium mines in Texas.

Continue on US 59 and you'll soon be back where you started. Stop in at the Skillet again, and savor the fun.

Highlights Along the Way

Guadalupe Wildlife Management Area. www.tpwe.state.tx.us/wma.

Aransas National Wildlife Refuge. Winter home (November–March) of the Whooping Cranes. Visitors center. Tivoli, 30 miles north of Rockport. 361/286-3559, www.wildtexas.com/parks/anwr.php.

Goose Island State Park. Brown pelicans and whooping cranes have been sighted at this 307-acre park on the peninsula between Copano and St. Charles bays. Also home of the Big Tree, an oak tree certified as the largest in Texas and estimated to be over a thousand years old. 12 miles outside of Rockport on Park Road 13 off TX 35. 361/729-2858, www.tpwe.state.tx.us/park/goose.

Corpus Christi.
USS Lexington: A floating naval museum in the vintage WWII aircraft carrier. The "Lady Lex" served longer and set more records than any other carrier. Tours of the flight deck, hanger, quarters, bridge, fully restored F-14 fighter and more. IMAX Theater on the ship. Adjacent to the aquarium, 2914 N. Shoreline Blvd. (Surfside exit from US 181). 361/888-4873, www.usslexington.com.
Selena Museum. Dedicated to the life and memory of Tejano singer Selena. 5410 Leopard St. 361/289-9013, www.selenaetc.com.
Corpus Christi Greyhound Race Track. Live pari-mutual racing wagering and simulcasts from Galveston and Miami. Full restaurant, lounge. 5302 Leopard St. 361/289-9333, www.corpuschristidogs.com.
Texas State Aquarium. 2710 N. Shoreline Blvd. (Surfside exit from US 181). 361/881-1200, www.texasstateaquarium.org.
Ocean Drive. Seven-mile drive along the Corpus Christi waterfront, bordered by parks and the seawall. Steps lead to the beach. Picnicking. Water garden at the bay-front Convention Center.

Goliad.
Goliad State Park: Replica of the 1749 Mission Espiritu Santo, interpretive displays, camping, picnicking, rest rooms. One mile south of Goliad off US 183. 361/645-3405, www.tpwe.state.tx.us/park/goliad.

Presidio La Bahia: Restored Spanish presidio (fort), museum with items from the Texas Revolution and artifacts from prehistoric civilizations in the area. Two miles south of Goliad of US 183. 361/645-3752, www.presidiolabahia.org.

Fannin Battleground State Historic Site. Where Col. James Fannin and his men surrendered to the Mexican army. Water, rest rooms, picnicking. Nine miles east of Goliad on US 59 to City of Fannin, then south on Park Road 27 for 1 mile. www.tpwd.state.tx.us/park/fannin.

Ride 22: Sun, Surf, and Sea
The Texas Coast to South Padre Island

The sun is shining and you are almost to Corpus Christi, the southernmost end of the Past and Present Texas ride. The only problem is that you are not ready to turn around and go home, and you don't want to brave the city traffic of Corpus Christi. You want to make this wonderful riding last at least a little longer. All you want is more of the fantastic riding you have just finished.

You are in luck, because not only can you ride a bit farther before turning around, but the riding gets even better.

Get ready to roll. The Sun, Surf, and Sea ride goes by mounding sand dunes and passes waves splashing onto the shore. Tropical Texas is the playground of snowbirds, retirees from the North who migrate here each winter, college students during spring break, and families from all parts of Texas and Mexico in the summer. This is the land of tanning oil, freshly caught fish, and beaches. Add in a motorcycle, and you have a sure formula for fun.

This ride starts in Aransas Pass, gateway to Mustang Island, one of the outer islands that fringe the Texas Gulf Coast and protect the harbors of the mainland. It features mile after mile of road flanked by dunes and beaches that make this a stunning place to ride.

In spite of all the "Life's a Beach" tee shirts everyone seems to be wearing, sometimes it's mandatory to go inland. On the way to the most famous and most rocking beaches in Texas on South Padre Island, this ride goes inland and passes through Kingsville, home of the famous King Ranch. The route includes long stretches of low-traffic road that are a sheer joy to ride.

Pack a bathing suit in your saddlebag for this ride. And don't forget to use the sunscreen. Even with a full-face shield on your helmet, the

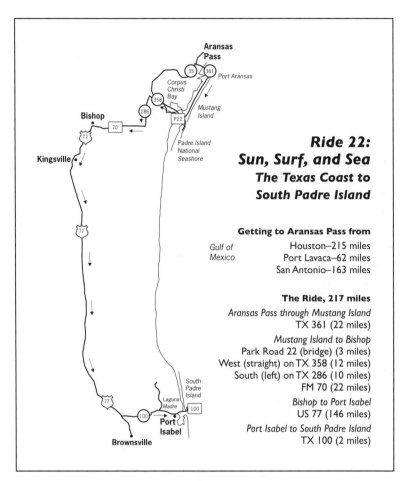

Aransas Pass

Port Aransas

Corpus Christi Bay

Mustang Island

Bishop

Kingsville

Padre Island National Seashore

Ride 22:
Sun, Surf, and Sea
The Texas Coast to
South Padre Island

Gulf of Mexico

Getting to Aransas Pass from
Houston–215 miles
Port Lavaca–62 miles
San Antonio–163 miles

The Ride, 217 miles
Aransas Pass through Mustang Island
TX 361 (22 miles)

Mustang Island to Bishop
Park Road 22 (bridge) (3 miles)
West (straight) on TX 358 (12 miles)
South (left) on TX 286 (10 miles)
FM 70 (22 miles)

Bishop to Port Isabel
US 77 (146 miles)

Port Isabel to South Padre Island
TX 100 (2 miles)

South Padre Island

Laguna Madre

Port Isabel

Brownsville

back of your neck and your nose might get burned. You will feel like you are in the tropics, so use caution when shedding clothes. Sleeveless shirts and halters might sound appealing, but the sun can burn no matter how fast you are going, and the bugs and birds don't care if they splat on your shirt or on your bare arms.

Technically, this ride is not difficult. Enjoy the long, uninterrupted stretches of sheer motorcycle ecstasy.

Getting Started: Aransas Pass through Mustang Island

By the time TX 35 coming south from Port Lavaca hits Holiday Beach and crosses Aransas Bay into Rockport, the landscape has already transported you into the tropics. Beaches, palm trees, and ubiquitous shell shops let you know that you are in a land of endless summer. This is the beginning of the Texas Gulf Coast at its absolute finest. The ships at the docks, oil storage on the shore, and normal businesses attest to the fact that regular people live and work here. For anyone on a bike, this is a land of riding bliss.

Stay on TX 35 as it becomes TX 35 Business through Aransas Pass. In the business district the road is still four lanes with a turning lane. At the fork, turn east (left), and at the dead end go right again onto TX 361. This will take you to the causeway that arches high over the Intracoastal Waterway to Port Aransas on Mustang Island. Even the name Mustang Island sounds like a wild place to run free.

Port Aransas calls itself "Saltwater Heaven." With the Gulf of Mexico lapping the Mustang Island beaches on the east and various bays less than a mile away on the west, this narrow island is surrounded by some of the bluest water in Texas.

Port Aransas is a pretty little town with lots of lodging, bait shops, and beaches for all the visitors who flock here. One of the most popular tourist destinations on the Gulf Coast, the town is filled with great places to eat that specialize in fresh seafood. In addition to the franchises are a number of mom and pop hotels and small bed and breakfasts. You cannot get lost here because there are just not enough streets to loose your way. The town and the entire island radiate a relaxed, laid-back atmosphere.

Keep going straight on the way to Port Aransas Park. You'll pass the Tarpon Inn, a vintage wooden hotel built in 1886. If you stay there, you will join the likes of Franklin D. Roosevelt and Duncan Hines as guests who have slept at the Tarpon Inn. You'll also pass the University of Texas Marine Science Institute Visitors Center. It has aquariums with Gulf marine life, movies, and other interesting exhibits. Then the road twists and curves some more on down to the beach. The sand is packed much harder on the right side of the fork, but whichever one you take, exercise caution. Also, expect glares from the fishermen if you get too close to the fishing jetty and rev your engine too loud.

After exploring Port Aransas, continue south on TX 361 to ride the entire thirteen-mile length of the island. If you time your ride for the off-season you may find yourself alone on the road, with only an occasional coyote or other wild creature to share it with. The two flat, straight lanes go through dunes sprinkled with sea grass, sea oats, and beach morning glories. There are frequent cutoffs to parks and beaches on both sides of the island. Mustang Island State Park offers five miles of seaside camping, swimming, shell collecting, and bird watching. The park also has picnicking, rest rooms, and showers.

Mustang Island to Bishop

At the end of the island you can cross over to the northern tip of Padre Island. But in just a few miles you hit the Padre Island National Seashore. After a few miles the paved road peters out. The protected area of the national seashore is in its natural state with no roads; not a good place to ride. Instead, turn west (right) onto Park Road 22 and head back to the mainland.

Park Road 22 becomes TX 358 on the Corpus Christi side of the high, arching, three-mile long bridge over the Intracoastal Waterway. The Corpus Christi Naval Air Station is on the right. If you want to see a little of the city, check out the Past and Present Texas ride.

Stay on TX 358 until you come to TX 286 and go south (left). After a few miles of super highway riding, follow the road as it turns west (right). Suddenly you'll find yourself on FM 70 on the way to Bishop.

Bishop to Port Isabel

The town of Bishop appeared on the south Texas prairie in 1910. The founder, F. Z. Bishop, laid out the business district and plowed under the grasslands to entice settlers to come. By 1912 Bishop had already sold more than 40,000 acres, and the town's population was 1,200. Many of these were Wends, descendants of immigrants from a particular part of Germany who originally settled near Bastrop. One of the more interesting customs of this ethnic group is that brides traditionally wear black. Evidently they knew even then what a well-dressed biker babe would wear.

Just a few miles down US 77 from Bishop is Kingsville, home of the famous King Ranch. In an area called The Wild Horse Desert by early settlers, Captain Richard King created the modern ranching industry in the mid 1800s. The first thing he did was to fence and clear his spread, ultimately 825,000 acres, an area larger than the state of Rhode Island. He developed a hearty stock of cattle, the Santa Gertrudis, and produced the first registered American quarter horse. The King

Ranch today is still a working ranch, with more than 60,000 head of cattle and 300 quarter horses.

To get a taste of life on the King Ranch, take the Corral Street exit off US 77 at the Visitors Center. Corral will curve around to take you to the King Ranch Gate. Just inside is the King Ranch Visitors Center. There are both historical and nature tours from the ranch. For a more eclectic view of days past, hook a left onto Sixth Street from Corral and stop at the King Ranch Museum. In addition to ranch exhibits, there are displays of guns, including a King Ranch Commemorative Colt Python .357 Magnum revolver and a collection of antique carriages and vintage cars.

The King Ranch Saddle Shop is a few blocks down on Kleberg Street. King began making saddles for his men more than 120 years ago because he could not buy the quality he wanted. Leather goods sold here are high quality and have prices to match.

Riding for the next hundred miles is on a four-lane divided highway that zips through the South Texas coastal plains, straight and flat. Make sure you leave with a full tank, so you don't hit empty during one of the long, lonely stretches with limited services. Lean back, relax, and enjoy the ride. You'll pass miles of pastures and a few fields as you travel through Sarita, Armstrong, and Norias before arriving at Raymondville. From here on are more of the services available that you might need. Harlingen, the next major town, has some real sights to stop for.

Harlingen displays more than thirty murals painted in and on buildings around town. The subjects range from depictions on the type of business housed inside to local history to Biblical themes. This is public art even a biker can love. The Texas Air Museum tracks the course of aviation and has occasional flyovers in antique planes. The Knapp Chevrolet Antique Auto Museum showcases vintage and classic cars, including a 1929 Chevrolet and a 1957 Belair convertible. For speed of a different sort, the Valley Race Park has live greyhound racing as well as simulcasts.

The Rio Grande Valley Museum consists of local historic buildings, including the Paso Real Stagecoach Inn built during the Civil War and the city's first hospital, stocked with vintage medical equipment.

Anyone staying overnight might want to visit Chuck's Icehouse. It claims to have the area's best Bloody Marys. Check it out in memory of Harlingen's most famous resident, the late Bill Haley.

Continue out of town on US 77 just a bit longer until you come to Park Road 100. To get to South Padre Island, take a left (south). Don't try to resist stopping at Little Graceland, a tribute to the "King" by Simon Vega, who was stationed with Elvis Presley in Germany. Also,

check out the race schedule at the Los Fresnos Motocross to see what's going on when you'll be flying through.

The cactus, palm trees, and yuccas are a reminder that, even next to the Gulf of Mexico, this is an arid area. In addition to being the Aloe Vera capital of the nation, where more aloe vera is grown than anywhere else, this is also one of the major citrus producing areas. You'll see both growing in fields along the way.

The road to Port Isabel has two lanes plus a passing lane. The Port Isabel lighthouse was used as a navigational light in the 1850s. In the first part of the Civil War, Confederates controlled

You can climb the winding staircase to the top of Port Isabel's lighthouse, the only one in Texas open to the public.

the lighthouse. When the Union tried to strengthen the blockade on Southern shipping, they took it over. At the nearby Palmetto Ranch, union and rebel soldiers fought the last battle of that war, more than a month after General Lee surrendered at Appomattox. Of the sixteen lighthouses on the Texas coast, only this one is now open to the public. Visitors can climb the spiral staircase to the top.

Port Isabel to South Padre Island

Although this ride has already crossed several fun bridges, this is the best of them all. It is two miles of four-lane highway over the deep-water channel. It arches into a high hill with a brilliant curve for a fantastic finale of great riding to a great destination.

South Padre Island is the host to the SPI Rally each fall. Whether or not you attend the rally, Padre Island is a place to kick back and have

Sand from the dunes drifts across the road on South Padre Island.

fun. At the foot of the bridge, turn right to go to Schlitterbahn Beach Waterpark and the end of the island. Turn left to head into town. Hotels, restaurants, bars, and shops line the main drag and fill almost every inch of solid land all the way to the water's edge on both the gulf and bay sides.

The commercial section seems to be constantly expanding north, but it does eventually come to an end. Here the riding is ripe for motorcycles. The two lanes appear to be carved out of the sand dunes, but the wind keeps blowing the fine granules over the concrete. Bits of beach try to cover the wide, paved trenches of the road. Sea grass waves in the wind coming over the dunes, making this last seven-mile stretch of desolate road feel like a ride on the moon. This is fabulous South Padre Island.

Highlights Along the Way

Port Aransas.
    Tarpon Inn: Vintage wooden structure from 1886. 26 rooms, seafood restaurant. 200 E. Cotter Ave. 361/749-5555, www.thetarponinn.com.
    University of Texas Marine Science Institute. Research facility with informative visitor center, Cotter Street, on the way to the beach. 361/749-6711. www.utmsi.utexas.edu.
    Mustang Island State Park. Almost 3,500 acres along the Gulf beach on Mustang Island. Swimming, shell collecting, rest rooms, showers, picnic arbors, beach camping, campsites with hookups. South of Port Aransas on TX 361. 361/749-5246. www.tpwd.state.tx.us/park/mustang.

Kingsville.

King Ranch. National Historic Landmark, birthplace of the modern ranching industry. Working ranch, nature and historical tours. Off TX 141, west of Kingsville. 361/592-8055, www.king-ranch.com.

King Ranch Museum. Ranch exhibits, antique coaches, vintage cars, saddles, etc. 405 6th St. 361/595-1881, www.king-ranch.com/museum.htm.

King Ranch Saddle Shop. Richard King began his own saddlery shop for the use of his men. Today the shop offers a variety of leather goods. 201 E. Kleberg St. 361/585-5761, www.krsaddleshop.com.

Harlingen.

Texas Air Museum. Aviation history from the early 1900s on. Occasional fly-ins and living history reenactments. FM 106, 1 mile east of Rio Hondo. 877-282-5777, www.texasairmuseum.com.

Knapp Chevrolet Museum. Antique and classic cars including 1929 Chevrolet, 1957 Bellaire convertible, several collectible Corvettes. US 83 at Stuart Place Road exit. 956/423-1370, www.knapp-chevrolet.com.

Valley Race Park. Live greyhound racing or simulcast racing. Food and beverages. 2601 S. Ed Carey Dr. 956-412-7223, www.valleyracepark.com.

Rio Grande Valley Museum. Exhibits include the Paso Real Stagecoach Inn built during the Civil War, Harlingen's first hospital with vintage medical tools, and others. Loop 499 at Boxwood and Raintree streets, www.theriograndevalley.com/museums.htm.

Chuck's Ice House. 1002 Morgan Blvd.

Little Graceland. A tribute to Elvis Presley that includes memorabilia, a replica of the Graceland gates in Memphis, and a model of his boyhood home. TX 100 East, Los Fresnos. 956/831-4653.

Port Isabel Lighthouse State Historic Site. Historic lighthouse/museum built in 1853. Spiral staircase to the top. TX 100 downtown at 421 Queen Isabella Blvd., Port Isabel. 956/943-2262, www.tpwd.state.tx.us/park/portisab.

South Padre Island. Riding on the mounds, grasslands, and mud flats is not allowed, but you can ride on beaches and roadways. Helmets are required. Remember, this is a resort area and people are on vacation. They may not watch for vehicles, so you have to watch out for them.

South Padre Island Visitors Center. Complete information about accommodations, activities and events related to seashore recreation. 600 Padre Blvd. 956/761-6433 , www.spionline.com.

Schlitterbahn Beach Waterpark. Slides, chutes, surfing on the beach. Restaurant and entertainment during the summer. South end of Padre Island. 956/772-7873, www.schlitterbahn.com.

SBI Bikefest. An annual October event. www.spibikefest.com

South Texas Plains

Just inland from the Texas Gulf Coast is the South Texas Plains region. Like all of the different regions of Texas, this one includes a lot of diversity. From the Rio Grande Valley to San Antonio on the north and the Gulf Coast on the east, the entire region is one of tropical weather and an enticing blend of the Spanish/Mexican along with the Texan. The food, the language, and the music all reflect this rich mixture.

The once small towns bordering the Rio Grande have now almost grown together along the major highway. But as you move west and north from the mouth of the river, the population thins and the towns are farther apart. The area encompasses great expanses of plains with long stretches of miles and miles of road and more road plowing through rich farm and pasture land.

This region stretches all the way north to San Antonio on the edge of the Texas Hill Country. As you travel north, you will begin to see indications of the differences. Towards the north and east of the South Texas Plains, this region borders on the Gulf Coast region. The South Texas Plains region includes many areas important to the Texas Revolution.

Only the Beach and Beyond ride is predominately in the South Texas Plains region. However, once the Past and Present Texas ride turns around to go back to its starting point, it travels through the historic South Texas Plains region when it passes through Goliad and Fannin.

Here you can enjoy long stretches of easy riding in a tropical climate. Even the winters are balmy and delightful for being outside and one with your bike.

Ride 23: Beyond the Beach
South Padre Island, the Rio Grande Valley, and Parts North

While the rest of the New World was still waiting to be discovered, long before the pilgrims arrived in Plymouth, Spanish conquistadors had already explored the Rio Grande Valley of Texas. Not finding the gold they were searching for, they left and did not return for another two centuries—the mid 1700s—to settle the land.

John Shary's vision changed the area from ranching to what it is today. He came to the Valley in 1912 and realized that the climate and soil were ideal for growing citrus. Shary was dubbed King of Texas Citrus. In the 1920s and 30s, he recruited experienced farmers from the Midwest to bring their agricultural know-how to the area. With the long growing season they could produce two crops a year. Now more than forty different crops are produced in this area, including cotton, all types of citrus fruit, sugar cane, vegetables, and melons. These are the main crops you will see as you ride by fields irrigated with water from the Rio Grande. Anyone who has ever eaten a Texas Red Grapefruit or a sweet Texas 1015 onion can appreciate the delicious produce grown in the Rio Grande Valley.

Ranching is still important in the area, but even that has changed. You are as likely to see ostrich or emu grazing in a field as cattle. You might also see antelope, bison, or even black rhinos. Keep your eye open for exotic creatures behind the fences and the less exotic varieties trying to cross the road.

This area is transcultural, with many influences coming from the Mexican side of the Rio Grande. The Spanish heritage is obvious everywhere you look, and it is still possible to easily cross the border into Mexico.

This ride takes you from the beautiful beaches and wildlife of South Padre Island, through some of the earliest landmarks of Texas history and on into twenty-first century economies. All this is done with a healthy dose of Mexican/Spanish influence and interesting roads.

This ride is one of the longest in the book. It goes from South Padre Island, where the Sun, Sea and Surf ride ends, along the Rio Grande and back to Kingsville. If this is a bit longer than you have time for, take one of the short cuts to go back north. No matter what you do, you will experience the vastness of the open road.

Getting Started: South Padre Island to Brownsville

Dust off your tires and kick the sand from your boots. As much as you may not want to, the time has come to leave South Padre Island and hit the road again. With only one way off the island, you have to leave

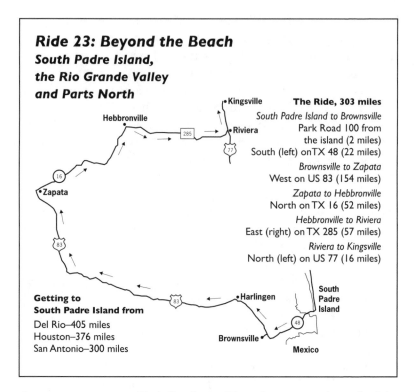

Ride 23: Beyond the Beach
South Padre Island,
the Rio Grande Valley
and Parts North

• Kingsville

Hebbronville

285

• Riviera

77

16

• Zapata

83

83

• Harlingen

Getting to
South Padre Island from
Del Rio–405 miles
Houston–376 miles
San Antonio–300 miles

Brownsville •

South
Padre
Island

48

Mexico

The Ride, 303 miles

South Padre Island to Brownsville
Park Road 100 from
the island (2 miles)
South (left) on TX 48 (22 miles)

Brownsville to Zapata
West on US 83 (154 miles)

Zapata to Hebbronville
North on TX 16 (52 miles)

Hebbronville to Riviera
East (right) on TX 285 (57 miles)

Riviera to Kingsville
North (left) on US 77 (16 miles)

the way you came, on Park Road 100. The ride starts at the end of the Sun, Sand and Surf ride (Ride 22), going over the high, arched bridge above shrimp and fishing boats in the water below. Once again you will pass the Port Isabel lighthouse. This is your last chance to explore the area before riding inland to tour along the Rio Grande River.

At the fork in the road, take TX 48 on the left side towards Brownsville. This is a good road, especially for a state highway, with four lanes plus a turning lane. Horses graze in pastures on the side of the road.

Once you get into Brownsville, stay on TX 48 and go straight on International Boulevard. This will take you by historic sights in the area.

Brownsville, "On the Border by the Sea," is the southernmost city in Texas. It officially became a city in 1846 after General Zachary Taylor established Fort Brown there. Placement of the fort was to confirm that the Rio Grande was the official border between the United States and Mexico. Unfortunately, building the fort triggered the Mexican-American War. Fortunately, relations have improved considerably since then.

Some original buildings from this early fort are now part of the University of Texas at Brownsville campus. The original hospital is now the administration building. The old morgue is just a short walk from the university library. The fort and the campus are on the left side of International Boulevard, just before the bridge that crosses the border.

The Brownsville Heritage complex, on the other side of the boulevard, includes history that goes back to the beginnings of Brownsville, from when the Spanish first came to the area on up to now. At the Gladys Porter Zoo, one of the top-rated zoos in the country, animals live in open exhibits surrounded by natural flowing waterways. Different habitats feature animals from different areas of the world: Africa, Indo-Australia, tropical America, and others.

Regardless of how many stops you make in Brownsville, take a brief detour through the old part of town to relish the Spanish and Mexican influence in the architecture and the atmosphere of the city. Then, for a dose of the real thing, go across the International Bridge into Matamoras, Mexico. Matamoras caters to visitors from the U.S. with lots of shops, markets, restaurants, festivals, and historic sites. Bargains can be found on handcrafted items. Some people even swear by the medical treatments available across the border. That is something you have to undertake at your own risk.

Brownsville to Zapata

Before leaving Brownsville, top off your tank. Fuel gets more expensive as you travel away from the coast. When you are ready to head onward for some more good riding, get on US 77/83 toward Harlingen. Cross International Boulevard and follow the signs to get on US 83 headed west. The longest highway in Texas, US 83 runs from the Texas-Oklahoma border in the Panhandle to Brownsville, a distance of 900 miles. There are only a few lights on the way out of town, so you will soon be following the meandering Rio Grande River. Even though there might be a little traffic on the two-lane road, there is no passing. Maybe a vehicle ahead of you will feel your impatience and pull over to the wide shoulder to let you by. Be extremely careful.

Much of the time you won't be able to see the river off to your left, but the path of the road will let you know it is still there. Between you and the river, in fact, on both sides of the road, are fields with native trees, shrubs, and cactus. If you see a field under cultivation it will prob-

Pull up here to get on the Los Ebanos ferry, the Rio Grande's only hand-drawn ferry.

ably be growing sugar cane, aloe, or one of the other Valley crops. This is citrus country, so you'll pass orchards and warehouses along the railroad tracks. It's nice to know where all that good stuff comes from.

About fifty miles west from Brownsville, US 281 crosses US 83. This is a good place to head north (right) if you need to ride towards home. Take US 281 the eighty miles to Falfurrias and you are almost back to the beginning.

Just after the intersection, you'll ride through Hidalgo. The city had to move inland when the river changed its course, or it would now be ruled by Mexico. The first international toll suspension bridge was built here in 1926. Palm trees lining the median between lanes of the divided highway for a while outside La Joya make this a pleasant strip to ride by. Priests in Mission are believed to have planted a citrus grove here.

Just outside of Mission is Los Ebanos, which has the only existing hand-operated ferry on the US-Mexican border. Follow the signs to the Los Ebanos ferry. To get there, you will go on TX 115 for about four and a half miles, then take a short jaunt on TX 241 to North Bridge Street. The blacktop road from the highway to the ferry meanders through orchards and a quaint community until it dead-ends at the river. The ferry carries three cars and a few extra passengers at a time. You can help pull, if you want. Don't be surprised if the ferry is not operating when you get there; hours of operation fluctuate. But if it's not running, you can at least stop and have a beverage by the dock.

Get back on US 83 and head on out towards Zapata. From here on out it's open road. Signs indicate that this part of your route is also part of the Texas Tropical and Birding trails. Because the road follows the river, it has lots of gentle curves. With few stoplights you can travel through the rural areas without having to worry about small town traffic. This is a road to zone out on and become one with your bike.

When you want to take a detour or break, you'll see all the franchises you know and love, as well as other places to stop. Fuel is available, but whether or not your particular type is available is another question. One thing for sure: it will be expensive. Fill up in Brownsville, or as early on the ride as possible. The farther west you go the more expensive it gets. Also keep in mind that the farther west you go the farther apart the towns are. That's great for riding, just not so great when you need to stop.

One interesting town is Rio Grande City, part of a 1753 Spanish land grant colony. By Texas standards, this is pretty old. Fort Ringgold, established in 1848, is one of the best-preserved military posts around. Robert E. Lee was stationed here before the Civil War.

Next down the road is Roma, which dates from 1765, although a Spanish mission was established here sixteen years earlier. The streets and homes look like Star Trek's Scottie beamed them straight out of Mexico. In fact, it looks so much like a town from the interior of Mexico that the producers of the movie *Viva Zapata* chose Roma as the location for outdoor scenes. There are traffic lights here, but it's a small town, so they shouldn't cause any problem.

Long, rolling hills take you away from Roma on the four-lane highway. You'll pass Falcon Dam and have picturesque views of the lake and pastures filled with mesquite and other scrubby trees. The road narrows to two lanes and becomes very isolated, almost eerie. Hunting is good here—deer, quail, dove, and more, depending on what is in season.

As you get closer to Zapata, the road goes back to four lanes again. This is a real city with many of your favorite motel chains. This is your last chance to zip over to Mexico before turning north. When you get into Zapata, you'll see the Plaza of the Flags from miles away. Use it as a beacon to go to the international bridge or to the monument honoring a local World War I hero.

Zapata to Hebbronville

Fill your tank before you leave Zapata, because it's another 51 miles to Hebbronville. There are a few towns between here and there, but there is a strong chance they won't have what you need. Turn north (right) onto TX 16 toward Hebbronville. Immediately you'll notice a difference in the terrain. The hills and gentle curves keep growing to remind you that these foothills are forerunners of the mountainous areas of Texas. The area is filled with wild critters that may wander onto the road, so watch out for them, dead or alive. Most likely you'll see at least a couple examples of road kill.

Around here they know how to mark hunting leases to keep interlopers out. The fences are high grids of wire that leave no doubt in anyone's mind that no one is to cross unless you belong on the other side.

Along this entire strip are native trees, shrubs, and cactus growing in the fields by the side of the road. Only a few houses are scattered between towns. One hazard to watch for is slow country drivers. But, on the other hand, you might not see any drivers at all. You will see the Border Patrol checking for footprints along plowed strips by the side of the road, or stopping suspicious-looking folks.

Hebbronville to Riviera

At Hebbronville, turn east (right) onto TX 285 and head toward Falfurrias. This is a town of only 5,000, but, after all the miles of empty land, it almost feels like a major city. The town was named "Heart's Delight" after a local wildflower, a romantic name for an important cattle-breeding center. Keep going through more beautiful pastureland until you get to Riviera. If you turned off on US 281 just before Hidalgo, you will meet up with this ride again. Turn east (right) onto TX 285 and finish the ride.

Riviera to Kingsville

Take US 77 North (left) toward Kingsville. If you came south on the Sun, Surf and Sea ride, you already know where you are. You are traveling in the opposite direction, but it is the same good road.

It's been a fun trip, long but fun.

Highlights Along the Way

Brownsville. Texas' southernmost city and the largest in the Rio Grande Valley, established in 1846 around Fort Brown. www.brownsville.org.

University of Texas at Brownsville. On the site of the original Fort Brown. 80 Fort Brown St. 956/882-8200, www.utb.edu.

Brownsville Heritage Complex. Home of the Stillman House Museum. 1305 E Washington St. 956/541-5560, www.brownsville.org/ MuseumHistory.asp.

Gladys Porter Zoo. Animals roam free in natural habitats. 500 Ringgold St. 956/546-7187, www.gpz.org.

Mission. Established by priests in the early 1800s. First citrus grove in lower Rio Grande Valley planted here. 956/585-2727, www.missionchamber.com.

Los Ebanos ferry. Only hand-operated ferry crossing the Rio Grande. Hours of operation are flexible. From Hwy 83 W turn south on FM 886 to Ferry Landing. www.playrancho.com/ferry.html.

Rio Grande City. Texas-on-line.com/graphic/riogrand.htm.

Roma. Founded in 1765 on site of an already-established mission. Resembles an authentic Mexican town. www.texasescapes.com/SouthTexasTowns/ Roma-Texas.htm.

Zapata. Early settlement on the Rio Grande. 956/765-4871, www.zapatausa.com.

Hebbronville. www.texasescapes.com/SouthTexasTowns/HebbronvilleTexas/ HebbronvilleTexas.htm.

Falfurrias. Name means "Heart's Delight," after a local wildflower. www.technidata.com/falfurri.htm.

Panhandle Plains

The never-ending stretches of unbroken horizon in the Panhandle Plains go on forever, and turn majestic shades of scarlet and gold at sunset. But bikers do not ride here merely to see brilliant sunsets. They know that one of the biggest myths about this area is that all roads are straight and flat.

Like the far West Texas rides in this book, if you don't live here you will expend a lot of time and effort getting here on your bike, trailering your bike, or renting one once you arrive.

Every bit of organization and planning will be rewarded with great riding and phenomenal views of canyons and topography that can be found nowhere else in Texas.

Here the thrill is not going up into mountains with twisty roads ascending to great heights. Here the thrill is going down into canyons below eye level on roads that have as much riding excitement as their ascending counterparts, but also having rugged, colorful strata majestically carved by a persistent ribbon of water.

These two rides go through different parts of Palo Duro Canyon, not far from Amarillo. Called the Grand Canyon of Texas, it is 120 miles long and twenty miles wide, stretching from the town of Canyon to Silverton. It reaches a depth of 800 feet from rim to floor, through bands of orange, red, brown, yellow, grey maroon, and white rocks representing four geologic periods. All of this was carved out of the rocky High Plains by the headwaters of the Prairie Dog Town Fork of the Red River, now a thin sliver of water at the bottom of the canyon.

These two rides pass through different parts of the canyon. Each ride is relatively short, so they can be combined into a full day of adventure. Enjoy the riding, but stop to fully marvel at the wonders of the area. If you get off the paved road and hike some of the canyon trails in the park, you'll get an appreciation of what the early explorers found.

The second ride cuts through private property, where you can stop only at the designated rest area. You will be in awe of the early engineers who created miracles in building the first roads through the rugged terrain.

In addition to the grandioso canyon, the panhandle of Texas celebrates both the cowboy heritage and freewheeling foibles of the state. So while you are here, ride on out to the Cadillac Ranch just west of Amarillo, where ten Caddies are planted hood-first into the ground, or enjoy a huge cowboy breakfast as the sun rises over the canyon walls.

Ride 24: Canyon Ride I
Palo Duro Canyon State Park

Palo Duro Canyon State Park is the only ride in this book totally inside the boundaries of a state park. A canyon of this magnitude is unusual, not just in Texas but almost anywhere in the world. Although other roads go through the canyon, they go through private property, where you cannot stop to hike, admire the strata, linger nor camp surrounded by the incredible canyon. There are things you can do in the park that you cannot do in private parts of the canyon.

One reason state parks are state parks is that they have scenic, historical, or ecological significance that is worth preserving. Riding within the park boundaries will expose you to a part of Texas more phenomenal and unusual than anywhere else in the state. You can hike or even ride horses down into the bowels of the canyon, closely examining all the strata, flora and fossils you can find.

In all honesty, however, there are some bikers who do not like to ride in state parks because speed limits are enforced. Others avoid the parks because of the fee charged to get in. This is one park definitely worth the fee. If you ride a lot, especially to places where there are state parks, the yearly pass is a very good deal. If you have an aversion to riding in a state park, try riding just this one. You will be rewarded with a thrilling ride through spectacular scenery. Otherwise, skip this ride and go on to Canyon Ride 2—the Untamed Wilderness ride. Both go through the Palo Duro Canyon, though each has its own perspective.

One of the great things about the Texas state parks system is that there are always directional signs from major roads pointing the way. So if you are on US 287/87, the road to Amarillo, follow the signs that guide you to TX 217 E and Park Road 5.

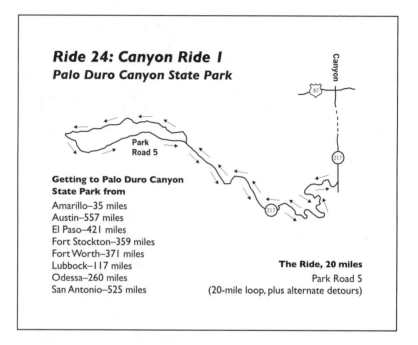

Ride 24: Canyon Ride I
Palo Duro Canyon State Park

Park
Road 5

**Getting to Palo Duro Canyon
State Park from**

Amarillo–35 miles
Austin–557 miles
El Paso–421 miles
Fort Stockton–359 miles
Fort Worth–371 miles
Lubbock–117 miles
Odessa–260 miles
San Antonio–525 miles

The Ride, 20 miles
Park Road 5
(20-mile loop, plus alternate detours)

Getting Started: Park Road 5

When the first thing you see upon entering the park is a sign warning of 10 percent grades for two miles and then a 90-degree curve, you know this is not a ride for sissies. There is no mistaking the message: this is going to be an adventure ride. Even though the basic loop through the park is only twenty miles long, these are some of most fascinating twenty miles you will ever ride.

The Park Road begins along the rim of the canyon with right-angle curves, sharp descents, and slow speed limits. Corkscrews on hills add to the challenge. The fifteen miles per hour speed limit in places is reasonable, even if this were not a state park. Park Road 5 demands low gears, caution, and, in places, possibly even brakes.

One sharp curve after another takes you down into the canyon. Even though you are going down, rather than up, the change in altitude may pop your ears. The opposite of flying has the same effect on your ears. Along the road are various scenic overlooks. Each one has a phenomenal view. Some of the side roads lead to hiking trails and campgrounds. Fortunately, the campgrounds all have restrooms that anyone can use. Sandwiches and snacks are available at the Trading Post and the Stables, both near the Sagebrush Camping Area.

As in all state parks, motorized vehicles, including motorcycles, must stay on the roadways. A number of trailheads have parking lots. Get off your bike at least once and stretch your legs on a trail. A word of warning—some trails allow horses. If you are hiking on one of those, watch your step.

Throughout the park there are six low-water crossings. Depending on the time of year and the amount of recent rain, these may not present a problem. If there has been rain, take these with care. Algae and slime can make the roadway slick, even if it is only under an inch or so of water.

In addition to campgrounds, the park also has a limited number of cabins. Staying overnight means you can watch *There are six low-water crossings in Palo Duro State Park. Cross them carefully!*

the glorious sunrise in the morning and also see the outdoor production of the historical musical Texas Legacies in the amphitheater at night.

The twenty miles of road are worth riding a second time; take the alternate route and go in the opposite direction for variety. The ride is exciting and the views breathtaking.

Highlights Along the Way

Palo Duro Canyon State Park. 11450 Park Road 5. 806/488-2227, www. tpwd.state.tx.us/park/paloduro.

Ride 25: Canyon Ride 2
Untamed Wilderness

One of the greatest natural wonders of the entire state is Palo Duro Canyon. As beautiful and majestic as the state park is, and as thrilling as it can be to be outside in the middle of the canyon, actually touching the strata of different colors and riding across the canyon from one side to the other makes an awe-inspiring trip.

One of the best places to do this is on TX 207, south of Claude toward Silverton. At this point, the canyon is about ten miles wide. For more canyon riding, turn around and ride it again. Taking hills and curves from the other direction is like riding an entirely new road; everything looks and feels different. Another option is to continue a bit further along TX 207 to the Tule Canyon for even more varieties of rock strata and more magnificent, sheer-faced, knife-edged buttes.

Unlike Palo Duro Canyon State Park, where you can wander along hiking trails and stop at civilized campsites, the land on either side of the road here is privately owned. Stop only at the roadside parks, scenic overlooks, and similar designated areas, where you won't be trespassing on someone's property. Of course, here you can enjoy the vistas and fantastic riding without paying the entrance to a state park; you just can't roam around as you can in the protected areas.

Getting Started: Getting to Claude

From Palo Duro Canyon State Park, retrace your route west on TX 217 until you come to the yellow blinking light at the intersection with FM 1151. Follow the sign towards Claude to the east (right). From Amarillo, take US 287 east to Claude. Exit at TX 207 going south. Claude may be twenty-nine miles away over what, initially at least, may not appear to be good riding. This is one time when looks can be deceiving. The two lanes start off straight with very softly rolling hills.

There is just enough topographical interest to make this good riding while still being easy and relaxing. Off to the side, just beyond the Black Angus cattle grazing in the pastures, there are faraway glimpses of canyon and what is coming next. While the road is basically straight and the land looks flat, it gradually increases in altitude. Along this stretch you are just as likely to pass another bike as you are to see cars, especially on weekends.

Or, if you are coming from Amarillo, take US 287 east to Claude. Exit at TX 207 going south.

TX 207 south of Claude

Turn south (right) on TX 207 at the intersection with FM 1151. The sign points the way to Silverton and the way to some of the most spectacular canyon riding anywhere. After about five miles, glimpses of canyon start to appear beyond the pastures and crops. Look toward the horizon to your right and you'll be amazed at the tantalizing hints of what is ahead. If you are not paying attention, you are likely to miss these little teases nature sends your way.

About this time, if you've met some other cars or bikes along the way, you'll be glad that a passing lane turns up periodically to help you get safely around the slowpokes. Though you know it is coming and you have seen glimpses of it along the way, the canyon seems to materialize instantly right before your eyes. Like magic, the canyon suddenly appears out of nowhere.

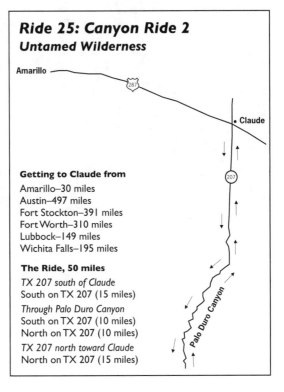

Ride 25: Canyon Ride 2
Untamed Wilderness

Amarillo

Claude

Getting to Claude from
Amarillo–30 miles
Austin–497 miles
Fort Stockton–391 miles
Fort Worth–310 miles
Lubbock–149 miles
Wichita Falls–195 miles

The Ride, 50 miles
TX 207 south of Claude
South on TX 207 (15 miles)
Through Palo Duro Canyon
South on TX 207 (10 miles)
North on TX 207 (10 miles)
TX 207 north toward Claude
North on TX 207 (15 miles)

Palo Duro Canyon

Through Palo Duro Canyon

This is the part of the ride you have been waiting for. The first indication of what is to come is the sign at the entrance to the canyon that says "Steep grade – 10 %, One mile," and then there is a curve with a 40 mph speed limit. Right away you know this is going to be great riding.

Add to this a deer crossing sign warning of critters your own size dashing into the road, then another 45 mph corkscrew curve; you know you are in for a real adventure. Although the hills are steep and the curves sharp, the hairpin turns are not on the steepest grades. The result is a fun ride that is not terribly scary, at least not for experienced riders

Palo Duro Canyon, one of the great natural wonders of Texas, is awe-inspiring as its changing contours are viewed from the seat of a motorcycle.

who exercise proper caution. Still, take this ride at a moderate speed, not just for safety's sake but also so you can absorb the incredible beauty of the canyon.

Be prepared to shift gears. The steep grades and sharp turns will demand it. You may even be tempted to use brakes on occasion.

The Prairie Dog Town Fork of the Red River lazily meanders along the floor of the canyon, daring those who do not believe this was the river's handiwork to search out other explanations for the magnificence of the canyon. The river looks so passive and harmless that you may find it difficult to believe that, with persistence and time, it created this amazing canyon.

The road through the canyon at this point follows a natural pass. It goes from the rim down to the floor and up again by following geological formations. The terrain on the side of the road is rugged and rocky with the potential for rock slides at almost every turn. If there has been rain or other severe weather, watch for rocks in the road.

Brilliant strata that change hues with the sun and shadows form bands of color along the canyon walls. Each epoch in geological time has its own signature. The most popular shades are red, explaining how the Red River got its name.

Almost at the end of the canyon run is a sign pointing toward a picnic area up to the left. Be sure to ride up the steep, curvy road to the overlook. The view is unbelievable, plus you will probably meet other bikers, so you can compare notes and comments on other places you have ridden.

Be prepared for high winds whipping around the canyon.

The end of the canyon is only a few miles further. Once you reach the flat, straight road heading south, turn around and go back from the opposite direction. The ten miles back across the canyon will seem like a completely different ride as you approach each curve, turn, hill, and formation from the opposite side.

Palo Duro Canyon to Claude

At the end of the canyon take a deep breath, stop at the rim, turn around and take a parting look at one of the greatest natural wonders of the state.

Then go north on TX 207 back through the miles of rich agricultural land to Claude, then to wherever else your heart desires.

Highlights Along the Way

Amarillo. Neither canyon ride goes through Amarillo, but if you are in the neighborhood and have the time, you might as well enjoy this area. All types of food, fuel, services, and lodging are available. www.visitamarillotx.com.

Cadillac Ranch. Ten Caddies are buried nose down in a field to represent the Golden Age of Automobiles from 1949–69. About 12 miles west of downtown Amarillo off I 40, exit Arnot Road.

Cowboy Morning/Evening. Mid-April to mid-October. Cowboy breakfast or dinner on the rim of Palo Duro Canyon. 800/658-2613, www.cowboymorning.com.

Helium Monument. A six-story stainless steel time column erected in 1968 to commemorate the world's largest deposit of this natural element. 1200 Streit Dr. 806/355-9547, www.dhdc.org.

Big Texan Steak Ranch & Opry. Offers a 72-oz steak dinner free to anyone who can eat the entire meal in one hour. Only about 20 percent of those who try succeed. Country/Western performances. 7700 I 40 at Lakeside. 806/372-6000.

Big Texan Cowboy Palace: Next to Big Texan Steak Ranch. Theater for concerts, special events and more. 806/372-6000, www.bigtexan.com.

Elkins Ranch: Chuckwagon suppers and Western entertainment, jeep tours of the canyon. TX 217 at Palo Duro Canyon. 806/488-2100, www.theElkinsRanch.com.

Buffalo Lake National Wildlife Refuge. A major waterfowl refuge area that's a winter haven for a million ducks and thousands of geese. Activities include an interpretive walking trail, a 4.5 mile interpretive auto trail also great for bikes, picnicking, and camping. FM 168, three miles south of Umbarger. http://refuges.fws.gov/profiles/index.

Palo Duro Canyon State Park. One of the largest state parks, including more than 18,000 acres of the canyon. A branch of the Red River has carved amazing spires and pinnacles and deep, plunging walls of multi-colored strata. Camping, picnicking, rest rooms and showers, interpretive center horseback riding, and hiking available. 512/389-8900, www.tpwd.state.tx.us/park/paloduro.

Pioneer Amphitheater: This is where the spectacular, award-winning historical musical Texas Legacies is staged during the summer, with the canyon walls as the backdrop. The show is preceded by a barbecue dinner and followed by a fireworks display. 806/655-2181, www.epictexas.com.

Canyon. www.canyonchamber.org.

Panhandle-Plains Museum: Twelve thousand years of human habitation in the Texas Panhandle is explored in the museum on the campus of West Texas A & M University. Exhibits also include the areas cowboy heritage and the Don Harrington Petroleum Wing emphasizing geology and the importance of the petroleum industry in this area. 2503 Fourth Ave. 806/651-2254, www.panhandleplains.org.

Index